A

P9-AGE-046

PS
3545
H16
Z88
1990

135316

N.L. TERTELING LIBRARY
THE COLLEGE OF IDAHO
CALDWELL, IDAHO

PURCHASED WITH NEH
ENDOWMENT FUNDS

Edith Wharton and the Art of Fiction

Edith Wharton, 1925. *Beinecke Library, Yale University*

EDITH WHARTON AND THE ART OF FICTION

Penelope Vita-Finzi

St. Martin's Press, New York

PS 3545
H16
Z88
1990

© Penelope Vita-Finzi, 1990

All rights reserved. For information, write:
Scholarly and Reference Division,
St. Martin's Press, Inc., 175 Fifth Avenue,
New York, N.Y. 10010

First published in the United States of America in 1990

Printed in Great Britain

ISBN 0-312-04187-X

Library of Congress Cataloging-in-Publication Data

Vita-Finzi, Penelope.
    Edith Wharton and the art of fiction/Penelope Vita-Finzi.
        p.   cm.
    Includes bibliographical references.
    ISBN 0-312-04187-X
    1. Wharton, Edith, 1862–1937 – Aesthetics.   2. Wharton, Edith,
1862–1937 – Technique.   3. Fiction – Technique.   I. Title.
PS3545.H16Z88   1990
813'.52–dc20
                                                                89-29480
                                                                     CIP

135316

To Cla, Adele, Sophie and Leo with love and thanks.

N. L. TERTELING LIBRARY
THE COLLEGE OF IDAHO
CALDWELL, IDAHO

Contents

Acknowledgements

I am indebted to London University for financial support for two years. I am grateful to Dr Cornelia Cook of Queen Mary College for much help and encouragement, my husband for his unfailing support, the late Professor Charles Peake for encouragement, Dr Roger Gard for advice, Dr Christopher White for helping to arrange my visits to Yale and I Tatti, and my children for their interest. I am also indebted to the Collection of American Literature, Beinecke Rare Books and Manuscript Library, Yale University, New Haven, for permission to quote material from the Edith Wharton Collection and the staff of the Library for their help, the Villa I Tatti Library, Harvard University Center for Italian Renaissance Studies, Settignano, Florence, and the monks of San Vivaldo monastery, Montaione in Valdelsa, Tuscany.

Introduction

Edith Wharton's life began in a well-to-do New York family in 1862 and ended in one of her two impeccable homes in France, Pavillon Colombe, near Paris, in 1937. At no time in her long career as a writer was financial necessity a motivating factor. The family and social position into which she was born, on the contrary, militated against artistic pursuits: she once said she was a failure in Boston because they thought her too fashionable to be intelligent and a failure in New York because they were afraid she was too intelligent to be fashionable. What, then, in the face of the prejudice and difficulties that stood in her way drove her to persist with the arduous life of a writer until she became a best-selling novelist and a Pulitzer prize-winner in her own time and an admired artist and a figure on a postage stamp in ours? She herself was interested from early in her career in the question of how a writer is made, particularly in how Edith Wharton the writer and her works came into being and from what sources her fiction sprang. Although it was not until the end of her life that she published her ideas about the writer in fictional form in *Hudson River Bracketed* and *The Gods Arrive*, drafts of a much earlier novel, *Literature*, exist among her papers in the Beinecke Library at Yale, and she publicly expressed her views in critical, travel and auto-biographical articles and in stories and privately in diaries, notebooks and letters. By studying all these sources, in particular the subject matter and evolution of *Literature*, *Hudson River Bracketed* and *The Gods Arrive*, a portrait of Edith Wharton the writer may be pieced together: her intentions, ideals and her view of the nature of her art and of the artist.

The figure in Edith Wharton's carpet stands out from her earliest published work to her last completed novels: order. Her ideal of order was found in traditional society and the art of the past. To her, the past provided precepts and models for living and for art. For the artist, personal and technical difficulties could be solved by adopting traditional solutions. Traditional society provided the structure that people – the artist at least as much as others – needed in order to function fully and progress. It also provided the richest material for the novelist, and traditional methods offered the surest basis for the art of fiction. In her travel books Edith Wharton used description of traditional cultures to express the aesthetic, moral and social values, classical in nature, which provided criteria for life and art and the basis of her method and of her themes in fiction. This belief in classical precepts informed her views on all aspects of life and art and led her to denigrate what she saw as anarchy in the modern world, in language and the novel, and epitomized by the New America. The formation of taste, a recognition of standards in art as well as in manners and language which was in her opinion notably lacking in America, was the aim of her earliest work *The Decoration of Houses*, her travel books, her theory and criticism, and a central theme in her fiction about the artist.

Edith Wharton's conscious conviction that order underlay all that was best in society and art meant that, when it came to describing and formulating a theory of fiction, the classical principles of proportion, decorum, harmony and form, achieved through conscious intention and selection, were inescapable. But her intellectual wish for rules and formulae to guide the writer could not override her intuitive knowledge of an inexplicable, subjective quality coming from an unknowable source within the individual artist. Artists, as she showed in her fiction, were born before they could be made, vital though their education was. Thus, in her theorizing on the art of fiction, she tends to fall between the two stools of dogmatic assertion and vague speculation. But it was perhaps her dual and, in many ways, contradictory nature that gave Edith Wharton much of her strength as a writer of fiction and softened the didactic tone of her recollections of life and travel.

The romantic side of Edith Wharton is discernible in the themes of isolation and loneliness in her fiction, in the importance she places on the longing for freedom in her characters, in her language and images in fiction and non-fiction, in her idea of the dual nature of artist and in her interest in the artist as a hero. It is also manifested in her view of the creative process as being charged by unconscious forces and an imagination developed and fed by human experiences. But those unconscious activities were always under the control of a 'guiding rational intelligence'. This view reflects a favourite simile of Goethe whom Edith Wharton greatly admired: that, like warp and weft, the interweaving of consciousness and unconsciousness formed the creative process.[1]

The negative aspect of her duality is seen in the way in which the precepts she laid down in her theory of fiction were often contradicted by what she stated as her practice, which, in turn, is contradicted by study of the way she actually worked. She is seen to be a meticulous craftsman in her ordering and planning although she maintained in *A Backward Glance* that she was, from early in her career, 'freed from the incubus of pre-designed plan': earlier in *The Writing of Fiction* she had expressed the need for rules and formulae for the writer. In fact, the manuscripts and drafts at Yale (her method for *Literature* is typical) show that craftsman and dreamer combined harmoniously in practice. She was less rigid in the application of precepts – at least in the art of fiction – than her dogmatic expression of them would imply.

The tension between reason and imagination, between the objective and subjective powers, that was a positive creative force for Edith Wharton was understood by her as such: and yet her disposition for harmony and discipline led her to want to resolve that tension. Not only did she explore in her fiction about the artist the concept of inspiration and the problem of its expression more deeply than she did in her own voice, but the tension between the artist's internal and external life provided central themes and plots. Her view of the artist as a unique individual with potentially anarchic powers was uneasily fitted into a theory of fiction and a world view which saw order as the ideal, but such conflict was perfect material for fiction. In fiction she was able to present her precepts for life and art dramatically opposed to her romantic, intuitive view of the artist's internal life and yet reconcile them. By showing the artist as having an innate gift of which he is unable to make full use until he has sounded his own depths and accepted his humanity as well as his genius, on the one hand, and until he has absorbed traditional culture and forms and learned that he must make concessions to society, on the other hand, she harmonized freedom with discipline and order. (For whatever reason, because Edith Wharton's artists are all men – with two exceptions (see page 154) – I have referred to the artist as 'he' throughout this book.) Conforming to traditional standards in art and in behaviour, as she did herself, allowed the individual freedom of the imagination, and allowed, finally, 'the gods to arrive'.

Edith Wharton's significance as a writer will, I hope, be illuminated by studying her views on art as expressed in her criticism and autobiography and as deduced from her books on travel and architecture, the evolution of her two novels about the writer, *Hudson River Bracketed* and *The Gods Arrive*, and the picture she portrays of the artist in other fiction. She is revealed as a complex artist deeply concerned with the nature of her art, and of the artist, and of the artist's relationship with society.

CHAPTER ONE

The Art of Living

In the works written in her own voice from the beginning to the end of her career as an author, Edith Wharton stresses the importance of order, in individual lives and in society no less than in art. From *The Decoration of Houses* published in 1897 to *A Backward Glance* published in 1934 her aesthetic values conform with the aphorism from Thomas Traherne's *The Vision* that she placed on the title page of *The Writing of Fiction* and at the beginning of her diary for 1924: 'Order the beauty even of Beauty is'.[1] She uses description of architecture, landscape, art and everyday life, to express her belief in the classical principles of order, harmony, proportion, discipline and absolute standards. Furthermore, these principles underlie her criteria for the art of fiction and they form central themes in her fiction.

In Edith Wharton's view this ideal of order is achieved by looking at the principles and practice of the past and applying them to the present. In *The Decoration of Houses* she affirms the classical axioms of proportion, order and simplicity belonging to a European past to counteract the stifling conventions of house decoration adhered to by Old New York: 'the dreary drawing-room' crammed with 'curtains, lambrequins, jardinières of artificial plants, wobbly velvet-covered tables littered with silver gew-gaws and festoons of lace on mantel-pieces' (*BG* 107). She also stresses the importance of fitness, of the suitability of a room to its function and to the creation of comfort: 'Here [i.e. with architecture and decoration] beauty depends on fitness, and the practical requirements of life are the ultimate test of fitness' (*DH* 196). The ideals gained from studying the past form taste and help in the 'complex art of civilized living'. She uses the past as a structure for the present as she does in formulating her theory of fiction; tradition and continuity for Edith Wharton underlie every aspect of life. As she points to the lessons to be learned by modern America from the underlying principles of Italian gardens and from the traditional structure of French society, so in *The Decoration of Houses* she and Ogden Codman are outlining and applying the lessons to be learned from German, French and, above all, Italian design, to contemporary decoration of homes.

The value of the book for a study of Edith Wharton is primarily as an expression of her classical principles but it also affords an example of practical application of those principles and a model of them in its style and structure. She expresses her ideals in clear, balanced prose within a book that is ordered in its arguments and its planning. Her proposition stated in the first chapter of the book is:

> that modern architecture and decoration, having in many ways deviated from the paths which experience of the past had marked out for them, can be reclaimed only by a study of the best models. (*DH* 2)

During the course of the book, the principles to be learned from this study are made clear. She sums up in the concluding chapter:

> The supreme excellence is simplicity. Moderation, fitness, relevance – these are the qualities that give permanence to the work of the great architects. . . . Much that is confused and extravagant, will give way before the application of principles based on common sense and regulated by the laws of harmony and proportion. (*DH* 198)

Precepts in house decoration are related to wider areas:

> If proportion is the good breeding of architecture, symmetry, or the answering of one part to another, may be defined as the sanity of decoration. The desire for symmetry, for balance, for rhythm in form as well as in sound, is one of the most inveterate of human instincts. . . . What the instinct for symmetry means philosophers may be left to explain; but that it does exist, that it means something, and that it is most strongly developed in those races which have reached the highest artistic civilization, must be acknowledged by all students of sociology. It is, therefore, not superfluous to point out that, in interior decoration as well as in architecture, a regard for symmetry, besides satisfying a legitimate artistic requirement, tends to make the average room not only easier to furnish, but more comfortable to live in. (*DH* 33–4)

Practical considerations are always important for Edith Wharton whether in the art of housekeeping, gardening, travelling or fiction. *The Decoration of Houses* exemplifies this practical side as well as her penchant for preaching. She and Codman divide the book into chapters each dealing with one of the component parts of a room – walls, doors, windows and so forth – and follow with chapters on each type of room – halls, dining-rooms and even nurseries. Every chapter contains some historical background, with photographs and good practical advice. For example, in the chapter dealing with fireplaces:

> Coal-scuttles, like andirons, should be made of bronze, ormolu or iron. The unnecessary use of substances which require constant polishing is one of the mysteries of English and American housekeeping: it is difficult to see why a housemaid should spend hours in polishing brass or steel fenders, andirons, coal-scuttles and door-knobs, when all these articles might be made of some substance that does not need daily cleaning. (*DH* 86)

The contribution of Ogden Codman, a trained architect and practising interior decorator, was, presumably, mainly to the technical aspects of the topics covered. Edith Wharton's 'cultivated sensibility' provided standards based on her European education and experience. The tone and content of *The Decoration of Houses* seek to educate taste and Edith Wharton's conviction that taste is formed through knowledge of the European past informs all her travel books and criticism and much of her fiction. The idea of education based on classical principles underlies her novels about the writer.

In *French Ways and their Meaning*, published in 1919 and written originally as a series of articles 'with the idea of making France and things French more intelligible to the American soldier', she declares:

> Real civilization means an education that extends to the whole of life . . . it means an education that forms speech, forms manners, forms taste, forms ideals, and above all forms judgement. This is the kind of civilization of which France has always been the foremost model: it is because she possesses its secret that she has led the world so long not only in art and taste and elegance, but in ideas and ideals. (*FW* 113)

For Edith Wharton *de gustibus non est disputandum*: her argument was with those who were ignorant of or rejected those values she knew to be right, and she sought to educate or convert. The four qualities she most admires in the French and that she considers lacking in American make-up are 'taste, reverence, continuity and intellectual honesty'. She defines taste as 'the recognition of a standard and states that: 'It is the regulating principle of all art, of the art of dress and of manners, and of living in general, as well as sculpture and music' (*FW* 40).

As in *The Decoration of Houses*, we are told in *French Ways* that 'the essence of taste is suitability . . . the word expresses the mysterious demand of eye and mind for symmetry, harmony and order' (*FW* 41). France is a model of taste from which 'a new people' can learn, in all areas of life: architecture, language, the theatre, argiculture, money-making, love-making, society, even manners (although she does admit at one point that 'the French too often economise manners as they do francs'). The cure for what she describes as 'taste-blindness' is 'the long slow old-fashioned one of education' (*FW* 53); the French eclipse the Anglo-Saxon races both in natural endowment of taste and in their belief 'that, to form, one must instruct' (*FW* 54). French education disciplines and strengthens the mind and preserves intellectual honesty in the same way that the rules of the French Academy preserve the standard of language and good manners, and traditional forms preserve standards in architecture and the planning of towns. When national danger threatens, it is this very discipline and rationality that gives France her strength. In *Fighting France*, her moving description of France at war, she declares:

> In great trials a race is tested by its values; and the war had shown the world what are the real values of France. Never for an instant had this people, so expert in the great art of living, imagined that life consisted in being alive. Enamoured of pleasure and beauty, dwelling freely and frankly in the present, they have yet kept their sense of larger meanings, have understood life to be made up of many things past and to come, of renunciation as well as satisfaction, of traditions as well as experiments of dying as much as of living. Never have they considered life as a thing to be cherished in itself, apart from its reactions and its relations. (*FF* 230)

This belief in the steadying influence of the past, in tradition and continuity as essential to individuals and art, is continually expressed. In a *Motor-Flight through France*, published in 1908, her reverence for 'the accumulated experiences of the past' pervades the account of her three journeys through the country that to her became a symbol of traditional values and the old order. Old buildings symbolize the past and traditional values which influence the lives of those who reverence them. In describing the order and harmony of the building Collège des Quatre Nations in *French Ways*, she is also extolling the values of the French Academy housed within. Eleven years earlier in *A Motor-Flight through France* a description of Georges Sand's house at Nohant became an expression of convictions:

> One beholds this image of aristocratic well-being, this sober edifice, conscious in every line of its place in the social scale, of its obligations to the church and cottages under its wing, its rights over the acres surrounding it. And so one may, not too fancifully, recognise in it the image of those grave ideals to which Georges Sand gradually conformed the passionate experiment of her life; may even indulge one's self by imagining that an old house so marked in its very plainness, its conformity,

must have exerted, over a mind as sensitive as hers, an unperceived but
persistent influence, giving her that centralising weight of association and
habit which is too often lacking in modern character. (*MF* 47)

To Edith Wharton, architectural form was symbolic of social and
moral order. This view is expressed as much in her novels as in her
non-fiction, and often more persuasively. Lily Bart in *The House of
Mirth* exemplifies the instability that lack of traditional ties and an
ordered background can lead to:

> She herself had grown up without any one spot of earth being dearer to
> her than another: there was no centre of early pieties, of grave endearing
> traditions, to which her heart could revert and from which it could draw
> strength for itself and tenderness for others. In whatever form a slowly-
> accumulated past lives in the blood – whether in the concrete image of
> the old house stored with visual memories, or in the conception of the
> house not built with hands, but made up on inherited passions and
> loyalties – it has the same power of broadening and deepening the
> individual existence, of attaching it by mysterious links of kinship to all
> the mighty sum of human striving. (*HM* 313)

Vance Weston has to learn to understand the past before he can fulfil
himself as a creative artist or a human being. The style of architecture
that gives *Hudson River Bracketed* its title symbolizes, ironically, the
Past to the raw boy from Euphoria but not to Halo brought up in an
older tradition. Ralph Marvell in *The Custom of the Country* begins
to appreciate the old values he had previously mocked once he has
come up against the vulgar new world: the contrast between the
values of the two worlds is symbolized by different styles of
architecture:

> Ralph Marvell, mounting his grandfather's doorstep, looked up at the
> symmetrical old red house-front, with its frugal marble ornament, as he
> might have looked into a familiar human face.
> 'They're right – after all, in some ways they're right,' he murmured,
> slipping his key into the door.
> 'They' were his mother and old Mr Urban Dagonet, both, from
> Ralph's earliest memories, so closely identified with the old house in
> Washington Square that they might have passed for its inner consciousness
> as it might have stood for their outward form; and the question as to
> which the house now seemed to affirm their intrinsic rightness was that of
> the social disintegration expressed by the widely-different architectural
> physiognomies at the other end of Fifth Avenue . . . what Popple called
> society was really just like the houses it lived in: a muddle of misapplied
> ornament over a thin steel shell of utility. (*CC* I, V)

Symmetry, simplicity, order are qualities she commended sixteen years earlier when she wrote *The Decoration of Houses* and that she was to extol over twenty years later in her autobiography. Edith Wharton's ideals remain consistent throughout her life although the expression of them becomes more peremptory as she strives to maintain that traditional values should continue to shape lives and art in an altered world.

In *The Decoration of Houses* and *French Ways* the intention is to instruct, and the author's principles underlie the advice. Clearly, in both books Edith Wharton is stressing the importance of tradition to civilized living. The past benefits the present firstly as an example of well-tried formulae: she says in *French Ways*: 'The quintessential is precious because whatever survives the close filtering of time is likely to answer to some deep racial need, moral or aesthetic' (*FW* 31). Secondly, it gives stability to individuals, to art and to society by providing a sense of belonging to a tradition: 'we should cultivate the sense of continuity, that "sense of the past" which enriches the present and binds us up with the world's great stabilising traditions of art and poetry and knowledge' (*FW* 97).

A Motor-Flight through France and *In Morocco*, ostensibly records of journeys through these two very different countries, are permeated, despite a disappointingly impersonal tone, with Edith Wharton's admiration for order and tradition. (She visited Morocco with Walter Berry in the summer of 1917 with the help of the Resident General there, General Lyautey, an acquaintance of hers to whom she dedicated the book.) Even when the monuments of the past have disappeared, tradition can be maintained through continuity of daily life, and the present can be enriched by the past. In *In Morocco*, published in 1920, a year after *French Ways*, she admires this unbroken chain of tradition:

> Nowhere else in the world . . . has a formula of art persisted from the seventh or eighth century to the present day; and in Morocco the formula is not the mechanical expression of a petrified theology but the setting of the life of a people who have gone on wearing the same clothes, observing the same customs, believing the same fetishes, and using the same saddles, ploughs, looms, and dye-stuffs as in the days when the foundations of the first mosque of El Kaiouyin were laid. (*IM* 263)

Throughout *A Motor-Flight*, published in 1908, description becomes an affirmation of her principles. Her thoughts on the cathedral at Amiens are characteristic:

> Yes – reverence is the most precious emotion that such a building inspires: reverence for the accumulated experiences of the past, readiness

to puzzle out their meaning, unwillingness to disturb rashly results so powerfully willed, so laboriously arrived at – the desire, in short, to keep intact as many links as possible between yesterday and tomorrow, in the ardour of new experiment, the least that may be of the long rich heritage of human experience. (*MF* 11)

Her belief that 'traditional society . . . is one of man's oldest works of art' (*GAN*) and that its order and restraints should inform all aspects of life colours her description of the countries she visits. The people of the Seine country:

> each had their established niche in life, the frankly avowed interests and preoccupations of their order, their pride in the smartness of the canal-boat, the seductions of the shop-window, the glaze of the brioches, the crispness of the lettuce. And this admirable *fitting into the pattern*, which seems almost as if it were a moral outcome of the universal sense of form, has led the race to the happy, the momentous discovery that good manners are a short cut to one's goal, that they lubricate the wheels of life instead of obstructing them. (*MF* 28–9)

Eleven years of living among the French modified Edith Wharton's opinion of French manners, as seen in *French Ways*, but her admiration for their sense of order, as she saw it, never changed.

From her descriptions of the countryside, life and ways of France and its monuments and cities, Edith Wharton is seen to be a travel writer of 'the cultured dilettante type' in the tradition of the nineteenth century. Her defence of the amateur approach is first made in *A Motor-Flight*:

> There are two ways of feeling those arts – such as sculpture, painting and architecture – which first appeal to the eye: the technical and what must perhaps be called the sentimental way. The specialist does not recognise the validity of the latter criterion, and derision is always busy with the uncritical judgements of those who have ventured to interpret in terms of another art the great plastic achievements. . . . There is hardly a way of controverting the axiom that thought and its formulation are indivisible, or the deduction that, therefore, the only critic capable of appreciating the beauty of a great work of art is he who can resolve it into its component parts, understand the relation they bear to each other, and not only reconstruct them mentally, but conceive of them in a different relation, and visualise the total result of such modifications. . . .
>
> Is there not room for another, a lesser yet legitimate order of appreciation – for the kind of confused atavistic enjoyment that is made up of historical association, of a sense of mass and harmony, of the relation of the building to the sky above it – deeper than all, of a blind sense in the blood of its old racial power, the things it meant to far-off minds of which ours are the oft-dissolved and reconstituted fragments? (*MF* 177–8)

Many years later in her autobiography, *A Backward Glance*, she reiterates her belief that 'there is certainly room for the gifted amateur in the field of artistic impressions – if only he is sufficiently gifted' (*BG* 142). By this date, 1934, 'the trained scholar' had taken over from the 'gifted amateur': Bernard Berenson had superseded Pater, Symonds and Vernon Lee[2] as the authoritative voice on art. Edith Wharton's own contribution to impressionistic travel writing and art criticism is fortified and given structure by her knowledge and sense of historical background, by her high standard of culture and by the skill with which she orders her impressions in her prose. Both her books about France are romantic in the sense that they are subjective responses to life and art, and classical in that they stress the importance of order, tradition, harmony, proportion and are written in a style that embodies these principles.

If *The Decoration of Houses* is clearly an argument for a return to classical ideas, it also contains a hint of the more subjective approach that was to characterize her subsequent work. Her two books about Italy, *Italian Villas and their Gardens*, 1904, and *Italian Backgrounds*, 1905, both written before the French books, demonstrate the classical and romantic sides to Edith Wharton's travel writing: *Italian Villas* emphasizes the classical principles; *Italian Backgrounds* is a subjective response to Italy, written in a more lyrical and impressionistic style than her other travel books, but revealing her predilection for order nevertheless. The former is an expression of aesthetic ideals into which her individual responses intrude: conversely *Italian Backgrounds* is a personal response to Italy's countryside and towns which she orders and assesses by framing what she sees through analogies with painting. In *Italian Villas* her classical side is leavened by the romantic, and in *Italian Backgrounds* the romantic is controlled by her classical inclinations. She preferred nature tamed by art, of the gardener or the painter. As selection gives meaning to the welter of existence in literature, so selection gives meaning to nature.

Italian Villas was intended by its author to be a serious technical treatment of the subject rather than an amateur approach. That this objective is not achieved entirely was not her fault. She was asked to provide a text for Maxfield Parrish's water-colours of Italian villas after the publication of her novel, *The Valley of Decision*, which established her credentials as a lover and scholar of Italy, and *The Decoration of Houses*, which established her architectural credentials. Unfortunately, as she admits in *A Backward Glance*, her 'articles were quite out of keeping with the Parrish pictures' (*BG* 39): these water-colours are impressionistic in style – 'brilliant idealisations of the Italian scene' (*BG* 138), whereas her text is mainly technical and scholarly. The editors refused to publish plans of the gardens and she refused to provide the editors with anecdotes and human interest. She comments retrospectively in *A Backward Glance*: 'if "The Century" wanted a series of sentimental and anecdotic commentaries on Mr Parrish's illustrations, I was surprised that one of the authors of "The Decoration of Houses" should have been commissioned to write them' (*BG* 30). The book nevertheless became a working manual for architectural students and landscape gardeners which was largely due to the professional text. In this book she is by no means approaching her subject in 'the sentimental way', but rather as an expert.

The stated purpose of *Italian Villas and their Gardens* was 'to describe the Italian Villa in relation to its grounds'. Her descriptions of the villas and gardens of Florence, Siena, Rome and its environs, Genoa, Lombardy and Venice demonstrate her scholarship and energy. But the book goes beyond description to instruction. She says in her introduction:

> There is . . . much to be learned from the Old Italian gardens . . . the garden-lover should not content himself with a vague enjoyment of old Italian gardens, but should try to extract from them principles which may be applied at home. He should observe, for instance, that the old Italian garden was meant to be lived in – a use to which, at least in America, the modern garden is seldom put. He should note that, to this end, the grounds were as carefully planned as the house. (*ItV* 11)

She admires the garden based on deliberate principles and planning, and, characteristically, draws a lesson from the past for the present. The past sets a standard which is not reached by the modern world. Although she admires the order and system of the old garden architect, she is never blind to the inspiration and imagination that inform any work of art. Indeed, she would give these prominence in the character of the artist in *Hudson River Bracketed* and *The Gods Arrive*. She concludes her introduction to *Italian Villas and their Gardens* – and the emphasis is on the gardens throughout – by saying that the real lesson to be learned is 'a sense of the informing spirit – an understanding of the gardener's purpose, and of the uses to which he meant his garden to be put' (*ItV* 13). The garden she was creating at this time at The Mount in Massachusetts bears witness to her ability to combine order and planning with imagination. Even today, the garden at the Mount, although reduced in size and only beginning to emerge after years of neglect[3], retains a sense of her 'informing spirit' as does the harmonious and beautiful house.

As can be seen from *In Morocco* and her French travel books Edith Wharton liked to see order in the landscape, but neatness by itself is seen as sterile: she dismisses Switzerland in *Italian Backgrounds* as 'an old maid's paradise that would be thrown into hopeless disarray by the introduction of anything so irregular as a work of art' (*ItB* 4). In this, the most ardent of her non-fictional works, she orders the Italian countryside by viewing it as art. The chapter that gives the book its title – the chapters were written at different times as a series of sketches – compares Italy with the Italian devotional pictures of the fifteenth century in that the foreground is dictated by the conventions of the art of the time, whereas in the background the artist expresses his personality and reflects his impression of the life around him. She continues:

> As with the study of Italian pictures, so it is with Italy herself. The country is divided, not in *partes tres*, but in two: a foreground and a background. The foreground is the property of the guide-book and its product, the mechanical sight-seer; the background, that of the dawdler, the dreamer and the serious student of Italy. (*ItB* 177)

Furthermore, in order to enjoy the painting, statues and buildings, 'they must be considered in relation to the life of which they are merely the ornamental facade' (*ItB* 178). Edith Wharton's view is that in Italy art so interpenetrates life that the traveller, firstly, must be familiar with the art of the past to understand the Italy of the present, and secondly, that art can give insight into the life of the past from which the art sprang. The first eight articles or chapters emphasize the first idea and the final chapter the second.

The serious student has to bring a high standard of culture with him to appreciate Italy – as does the reader to *Italian Backgrounds*:

> One must know Titian and Giorgione to enjoy the intimacy of the Friulian Alps, Cima de Conegliano to taste the full savour of the strange Euganean landscape, Palladio and Sansovino to appreciate the frivolous villa-architecture of the Breta, nay, the domes of Brunelleschi and Michael Angelo to feel the happy curve of some chapel cupola in a nameless village of the hills. (*ItB* 178)

Edith Wharton uses analogies with the work of architects and painters to convey the quality of the scene she wishes to describe. For example, she describes the view from the hills behind Biella by saying that it 'suggests some heroic landscape of Poussin's, or the boundless russet distances of Rubens's "Château of the Stein" '(*ItB* 48). With the view towards Orvieto, the landscape is not only evoked by reference to Turner's 'Road to Orvieto' but is given significance: Turner's art, by 'summing up and interpreting the spirit of the scene', has given to the traveller a new vision so that 'pausing by the arched bridge above the valley he loses sense of the boundaries between art and life, and lives for a moment in that mystical region where the two are one' (*ItB* 146). She employs allusions to paintings as a descriptive shorthand and to convey 'the underlying spirit of Italy', for the painter – or at least he who possesses 'the seeing soul' – does not merely copy what he sees but transmutes it through creative vision into art which communicates ideas and emotions behind appearances. Art and life become one in contemplation of a scene familiar from a painting, or when the scene is illuminated by reference to art. In particular, the great masterpieces of Italy 'hold the key to some secret garden of the imagination' and without the necessary education the traveller cannot get beyond the foreground or the guidebook Italy.

The educated traveller must not, however, be only academic. His knowledge of the past and appreciation of the art of Italy as part of a great tradition must not restrict him to looking at paintings, statues and buildings as museum pieces. They must be contemplated as part of the life from which they sprang and this can be seen and understood by looking behind the foreground figures in fifteenth-century paintings or by turning to contemporary literature and paintings of later periods. She commends Goldoni's plays and Longhi's paintings because 'both were content to reflect, in the mirror of a quietly humorous observation, the everyday incidents of the piazza, the convent and the palace' (*ItB* 204). Even inferior works can be valuable as records of everyday life: a novel by Scudo succeeds in reproducing the atmosphere of eighteenth-century Venice. He does this 'not by force of talent but by the patient accumulation of detail' (*ItB* 211). Her interest in the details of manners and customs of the past displays her belief in 'character first of all as a product of particular material and social conditions' (*WF* 7) and her own method in her novels, particularly her historical novels, shows her to be meticulous over the details of everyday life – to such an extent in *The Valley of Decision*, set in eighteenth-century Italy, that the background overwhelms the characters and narrative. Edith Wharton sees a concern with describing scenes and manners as essential to the historical novelist in particular; she derides Georges Sand for ignoring background material which, she says scathingly, is 'so alien to the "romantic" conception of life' (*ItB* 212). (Certainly the excesses of the Romantic movement as construed by Georges Sand were alien to Edith Wharton.) The 'historical imagination' – that is, the ability to imagine an earlier age and to re-create it – is fed by the minutiae of the common round. As art springs from the conditions of life surrounding the artist, it is by looking at the details of everyday life in the work that we can understand more about both the art and the contemporary scene. If the student can realize this, he will free himself from the attitude of the 'guide-book tourist' who only looks at what he has been told to admire and begin

to understand and to sympathize with the different modes in which man has sought to formulate his gropings after beauty. . . . To enjoy any form of artistic expression one must not only understand what it tries to express, but know
The hills where its life rose,
And the sea where it goes. (*ItB* 184)

Edith Wharton admires the French for the way in which they make every aspect of life an art, and Italy because so much remains as part of life in the present as it was represented in the art of the past: the traveller can 'see what horizons the old masters looked out on, and note that the general aspect of the country is still almost as unchanged as the folds of the Umbrian mountains and the curves of the Tuscan streams' (*ItB* 176). Continuity in itself gives aesthetic satisfaction to Edith Wharton, as does 'the Latin ideal [which] demanded space, order, and nobility of composition'.

The order that Edith Wharton can be seen from her travel books to admire in 'traditional society, with its old-established distinctions of class, its passwords, exclusions, delicate shades of language and behaviour' (GAN), became the rule in her own life. She writes in a letter to Bernard Berenson: 'I esteem order above every gift and virtue.'[4] To her friends this admiration for order was manifest in her life. Nicky Mariano in describing Edith Wharton's house at Sainte-Claire, Hyères, in her book *Forty Years with Berenson*, writes:

A terraced garden all around and above the house, beautifully kept, almost too much so. A certain wildness and *laissez-aller* would have been more in harmony with the landscape. But the orderliness of the garden corresponded to the exquisitely furnished and appointed rooms and to the definite and strict ritual that regulated the house's daily life. (1966, 162)

To some of her friends her addiction was daunting. Madame Saint-René Tallandier, who was part of a circle in France which 'represented what she most appreciated in our old traditional France', writes in her contribution to Percy Lubbock's *Portrait of Edith Wharton*:

The perfection of her taste, extending to everything, even to the smallest details of her establishment, the arrangement of the flower-beds, the symmetry of the hedges, the neat ranks of the trees in the orchard – sometimes, when I was too conscious of it all, it chilled me. . . . I have often noticed, among Americans attracted by our civilization and our traditions, something for which we ourselves are scarcely prepared, something that exceeds our measure – almost, in the English phrase, 'too much of a good thing'. With Mrs Wharton I was intimidated by the aesthetic perfection of everything about her. (PL 152)

Percy Lubbock himself adopts a tone of affectionate mockery when he describes her making the rounds of the garden at Sainte-Claire:

> Discipline, as ever, was strict; she would have no shirking or sulking, and it was a stupid little plant that ever dreamed of dodging her eye. But it was a fine life for honest effort; liberty, so you know how to use it, was the note of the garden, adventure when you have learnt control. (PL 169)

Charles du Bos, who contributes the most sensitive and affectionate view of her to the *Portrait*, comments:

> Everything and everybody was placed by her where it should be placed, related to the never disturbed and never forgotten background of the great traditional references; and in that respect nothing is more revealing than the admirable sentence of Traherne that she chose as a motto for *The Writing of Fiction*, 'Order the beauty even of Beauty is'. Anarchy under any form, but most of all anarchy of judgement, was abhorrent to her. (PL 98)

The same quotation is written in her handwriting on the second page of her diary/notebook of 1924 onwards under the heading 'My Motto' and after a note on the previous page: 'If ever I have a biographer it is in these notes that he will find the gist of me.'

The intimidating old woman insistent on obedience to her domestic discipline originates in the conscientious child with the 'old obediences' in her blood brought up in Old New York. In the society that she depicts in *A Backward Glance* and 'A Little Girl's New York' and in *The Age of Innocence*, the four Old New York novellas, and other fiction, she shows that Old New York made habits and rules into virtues, and created a monotonous and provincial society where 'beauty, passion and danger were automatically excluded' and where 'the tepid sameness of the moral atmosphere resulted in a prolonged immaturity of mind' (*LGNY*). But in looking back on her parents' world she concludes, as she shows Ralph Marvell doing, that the advantages of their standards outweighed the irritations and restrictions of convention. Although 'the weakness of the social structure of my parents' day was a blind dread of innovation and an instinctive shrinking from responsibility' (*BG* 22), its strength lay in 'the concerted living up to long-established standards of honour and conduct, of education and manners' (*BG* 5).

The discipline imposed on her as a child and the standards set for her influenced her values throughout her life. Although she can see that 'conformity is the bane of middle-class communities' (*BG* 23) and Percy Lubbock tells us that 'the vials of her sarcasm' were never more liberally discharged than 'on the claims and assumptions of that same honourable tradition [i.e. the French] when it is not the past that rules it with a living spirit, but convention with a dead hand' (PL 159), she belongs by nature and nurture to a world where adherence to traditional principles of order, reason, discipline and harmony pertain. From the beginning of her career as a writer in *The Decoration of Houses* to nearing its end in *A Backward Glance*, she asserts her belief in these principles and in the traditional civilizations that preserve and value them in social forms, in individual lives and in art.

Her beliefs, which crystallized with age and faced with a world dislocated from the old order by the war, inevitably led her towards denigration of the modern world, its values and its art. But from the beginning she expresses disapproval of contemporary decline as she saw it, from the standards of the past, particularly in America. *The Decoration of Houses* is a treatise on the virtues of the past:

> Modern civilization has been called a varnished barbarism: a definition that might well be applied to the superficial graces of much modern decoration. Only a return to architectural principles can raise the decoration of houses to the level of the past. (*DH* 198)

Almost every aspect of modern American decoration is gently derided for its 'architectural vagaries'. As she was to symbolize social disintegration by architectural structures in *The Custom of the Country*, so in *The Decoration of Houses* she declares, in an attack on central heating, that 'it might almost be said that the good taste and *savoir-vivre* of the inmates of a house might be guessed from the means used for heating it' (*DH* 87). Seven years later the derision begins to be less gentle: in *Italian Villas and their Gardens*, she talks of 'the haphazard and slipshod designs of the present day' (*ItV* 250). Her admiration for the landscape and monuments of France expressed in *A Motor-Flight through France* often leads her to disparagement of her native land 'which has undertaken to get on without the past, or to regard it only as a "feature" of aesthetic interest, a sight to which one travels rather than a light by which one lives' (*MF* 11). Even physiognomy has deteriorated in the democratic age:

> We live in the day of little noses: that once stately feature, intrinsically feudal and aristocratic in character – the *maschio naso* extolled of Dante – has shrunk to democratic insignificance, like many another fine expression of individualism. . . . And so the deterioration has gone on from generation to generation, till the nose has worn itself blunt against the increasing resistances of a democratic atmosphere, and stunted, atrophied and amorphous, serves only, now, to let us know when we have the influenza. (*MF* 22)

By 1919 in *French Ways and their Meaning*, America epitomizes all that is wrong with the modern world. Edith Wharton feels that America is throwing away her inheritance from the European tradition:

> America is now ripe to take her share in the long inheritance of the races she descends from; and it is a pity that just at this time the inclination of the immense majority of Americans is setting away from all real education and culture. (*FW* 72)

Lack of appreciation for this tradition and indifference to the ideals in life and art stemming from it are reflected in many aspects of life and literature. Attitudes towards money in particular are seen as revealing a basic dissimilarity in comparison with France, her model of order and tradition: 'Americans are too prone to consider money-making as interesting in itself: they regard the fact that a man has made money as something intrinsically meritorious' (*FW* 107). She links the attitude towards money-making with the American attitude towards culture:

> Every sham and substitute for education and literature and art had steadily crowded out the real thing. 'Get-rich-quick' is a much less dangerous device than 'get-educated-quick', but the popularity of the first has led to the attempt to realise the second. It is possible to get rich quick in a country full of money-earning chances; but there is no short-cut to education. (*FW* 72)

In Edith Wharton's view the rapid material prosperity available to the American encourages intellectual laziness and perpetual immaturity. She makes this point ten years later in *Hudson River Bracketed* and *The Gods Arrive* in the satirical portrait she paints of Vance's home life in Euphoria.

An entire chapter of *French Ways* is devoted to 'the New French woman' for whom Edith Wharton has little but praise and in contrast with whom her American counterpart comes off badly: 'Compared with the women of France the average American woman is still in the kindergarten' (*FW* 101). The reason for this immaturity is that the American woman lives in a world cut off from 'real living':

> Real living . . . is a deep and complex and slowly developed thing, the outcome of an old and rich social experience. It cannot be 'got up' like gymnastics, or a proficiency in foreign languages, it has its roots in the fundamental things, and above all in close and constant and interesting and important relations between men and women. (*FW* 102)

Lack of 'frank and free' social relations between the sexes 'has done more than anything else to retard real civilization in America' (*FW* 113). Because the American woman lacks involvement with every aspect of life including business she remains a child and this prevents the development of 'real civilization' 'where the power of each sex is balanced by that of the other' (*FW* 113), whereas 'as life is an art in France, so woman is the artist' (FW 112).

Art and civilization are founded on traditional order and standards in manners, morality, education, ideas and ideals, painting and sculpture, architecture, literature and language. Above all, Edith Wharton disliked anarchy in language and literature and America epitomizes this lack of order:

> The lover of English need only note what that rich language has shrunk to on the lips, and in the literature, of the heterogeneous millions of American citizens who, without uniformity of tradition or recognised guidance, are being suffered to work their many wills upon it. (*FW* 50)

America has 'the magnificent, the matchless inheritance of English speech and English letters' (*FW* 96) but she has not appreciated the value of continuity and tradition, or:

> she would have kept a more reverent hold upon this treasure, and the culture won from it would have been an hundredfold greater. She would have preserved the language instead of debasing and impoverishing it; she would have learned the historic meaning of its words instead of wasting her time inventing short-cuts in spelling them; she would jealously have upheld the standards of its literature instead of lowering them to meet an increased 'circulation'. (*FW* 97)

As she relates in *A Backward Glance*, although she was brought up in a society where the arts were non-existent and authorship regarded as 'something between a black art and a form of manual labour' (*BG* 69), this same society set standards not only in manners and morality, but in speaking English:

> usage, in my childhood, was as authoritative an element in speaking English as tradition was in social conduct. And it was because our little society still lived in the reflected light of a long-established culture that my parents, who were far from intellectual, who read and studied not at all, nevertheless spoke their mother tongue with scrupulous perfection, and insisted that their children should do the same.
> . . . it would have been 'bad manners' to speak 'bad' English, and 'bad manners' were the supreme offence. (*BG* 48–52)

Similarly, her father's 'gentleman's library', although largely unread
except by her, represented a standard against which her mother
would measure the works of fiction that her daughter had to present
to her for an approval that was almost always withheld. Here she is
looking back to a vanished world of Old New York which lived
rigidly by the traditions of its European inheritance and over which
nostalgia casts a rosy glow from a world where she considered that an
increasing decline in language and literature had been taking place.

To Edith Wharton, a degeneration in America of standards in
language is mirrored in its everyday life. In an article for *The Yale
Review*, written in 1927, with the ironic title of 'The Great American
Novel', she declares:

> In inheriting an old social organization which provided for nicely shaded
> degrees of culture and conduct, modern America has simplified . . . it out
> of existence, forgetting that in such matters the process is necessarily one
> of impoverishment. As she has reduced the English language to a mere
> instrument of utility . . . so she has reduced relations between human
> beings to a dead level of vapid benevolence, and the whole of life to
> a small house with modern plumbing and heating, a garage, a motor, a
> telephone, and a lawn undivided from one's neighbour's.

Literature too has been impoverished by the move away from
European tradition and society. By limiting itself to the American
scene where 'it must tell of persons so limited in education and
opportunity that they live cut off from all the varied sources of
culture which used to be considered the common heritage of English-
speaking people' the contemporary American novel is judged by
Edith Wharton to be doomed. As she sees it, American society offers
'the artist's imagination a surface as flat and monotonous as our own
prairies' and therefore the art springing from such surroundings must
inevitably be lacking in depth. On the other hand 'the dense old
European order, all compounded of differences and nuances, all
interwoven with intensities and reticences, with passions and privacies'
provides a rich and varied subject matter for the novelist. She scorns
in particular 'the idea that genuineness is to be found only in the
rudimentary and that whatever is complex is unauthentic' and that
'the modern American novelist is told that the social and educated
being is an unreality unworthy of his attention, and that only the man
with the dinner-pail is human'. To Edith Wharton the conditions of
life in America could not produce great art; 'the great American
novel' was an impossibility by 1927.

Her vision of the future of the novel was one firmly based on the
principles of the past: 'a past full enough for the deduction of certain
principles'. The novelists of the past from whom she deduces these

principles are, it seems, Balzac, Jane Austen, Tolstoy and Thackeray – whom she describes in her article 'The Vice of Reading' in 1903 as 'the four greatest life-givers' – Flaubert, Stendhal, George Eliot, and with certain reservations, Hardy, Trollope, Samuel Butler, Richardson, Sterne, Smollett, Fielding and Meredith. Percy Lubbock, in describing what she enjoyed for an evening's reading, tells us that:

> Scott could never be admitted, nor Dickens either, incorrigible monsters; there was no more to be said – she saw only their crimes. Thackeray . . . could be indulged for a time, supreme while it lasted, till he too was in disgrace for his sentimental frailties . . . are there any who are beyond reproof? . . . Jane Austen, of course, wise in her neatness, trim in her sedateness; she never fails, but there are few or none like her. There is George Eliot indeed, who may have her faults, but even Edith, for old sake's sake, as in filial tenderness, could be blind to these – righting the balance by curt dismissal of Charlotte Brontë . . . Edith could always settle back in her corner, comfortable and approving, to attend, if you please, to the ambling chronicles of Trollope. (PL 173)

Yet, when she is writing seriously rather than entertaining friends, she appreciates the strengths of Scott, Dickens and Thackeray. The novelists of her day who disregard all previous methods and criteria appear to her to offer nothing in their place. She asserts in 'Tendencies in Modern Fiction', that censorious look at the postwar novel written in 1934, that:

> The moral and intellectual destruction caused by the war, and by its far-reaching consequences, was shattering to traditional culture; and so far as the new novelists may be said to have any theory of their art, it seems to be that every new creation can issue only from the annihilation of what preceded it. But the natural processes go on in spite of theorizing, and the accumulated leaf-mould of tradition is essential to the nurture of new growths of art.

This view she had expressed at the beginning of her career in *The Decoration of Houses*:

> Thus, in reasoning, originality lies not in discarding the necessary laws of thought, but in using them to express new intellectual conceptions; in poetry, originality consists not in discarding the necessary forms of rhythm, but in finding new rhythms within the limits of those laws. (*DH* 9)

In *The Writing of Fiction*, published in 1924, she repeats this belief: 'True originality consists not in a new manner but in a new vision' (*WF* 18).

It is not surprising, given her belief in the importance of traditional values for society and of standards in language and literature based on past forms, that her opinion of the contemporary novel in the early part of this century should be scathing. Her definition of the novel 'to the generation which read Dickens and Thackeray, Balzac and Stendhal' in the article 'Permanent Values in Fiction' (1934) as 'a work of fiction containing a good story about well-drawn characters' inevitably distances her from many of her contemporaries. In 'Tendencies in Modern Fiction' written also in 1934, she asserts:

> The novelists most in view reject form not only in the structure of their tales but in the drawing of character. They reduce to the vanishing point any will to action, and their personages are helpless puppets on a sluggish stream of fatality.

On the whole she restricts her derision in print to general comment, although she names Virginia Woolf, James Joyce and D.H. Lawrence in 'Permanent Values in Fiction'. She calls Lawrence's characters 'no more differentiated than a set of megaphones, through all of which the same voice interminably reiterates the same ideas'. Of *Ulysses* she had written to Bernard Berenson 'It's a turgid welter of pornography (the rudest schoolboy kind), and uninformed and unimportant drivel.'[5] With her belief 'that any lasting creative work must be based on some sort of constructive system' (*TMF*) she was unable to appreciate experiments with form in the novel or with the portrayal of character. She feels that 'the trend of the new fiction, not only in America and England, but on the continent, is chiefly toward the amorphous and the agglutinative' (*TMF*). In both 'Tendencies to Modern Fiction' and 'Permanent Values in Fiction', written within four years of her death when she was over seventy, she ends her diatribe against the lack of structure in the contemporary novel, against 'the chaos of present conditions in life and art', by asserting her belief that what will prove to be of permanent value in the novel is the ability to create living characters and to tell a story.

Traditional culture provides the richest material for the novelist: 'Balzac's provincial France, Jane Austen's provincial England . . . made up for what they lacked in surface by the depth of the soil in which they grew. This is indeed still true of the old European order' (*GAN*). Traditional methods too are basic to her concept of the art of fiction; for these she admires Proust above all her contemporaries: 'The more one reads of Proust the more one sees that his strength is the strength of tradition. All his newest and most arresting effects have been arrived at through the old way of selection and design' (*WF* 154). She devotes a whole chapter to Proust in *The Writing of Fiction*, commending him particularly for his ability to create living characters and to make their destinies seem inevitable, as well as his skill in employing old methods towards conveying a new vision.

She also admires Sinclair Lewis – 'he really *is* an artist'[6] – for his ability to create 'living people' who are 'embodied in consecutive and significant narrative'. Among contemporary novels she admires are Scott Fitzgerald's *The Great Gatsby* – which was published the same year as one of her weakest novels *The Mother's Recompense* – Dreiser's *An American Tragedy*, William Gerhardi's *Futility*, Dos Passos's *Manhattan Transfer*, Willa Cather's *The Professor's House*, Alberto Moravia's *Gli Indifferenti*, and, strangely, given her scorn of the novel of ideas, Aldous Huxley's *Brave New World*, as well as *Antic Hay* and *Those Barren Leaves*. (Huxley and his wife became her neighbours on the Riviera in 1930 and thereafter visited her in her villa at St Hyères from time to time.)[7] She also approves of George Santayana's novel *The Last Puritan*, some of Somerset Maugham's stories, Anita Loos's *Gentlemen Prefer Blondes*, Colette's work,[8] and a small selection of scenes in Henry James's novels, although her admiration for his work, particularly the later novels, is reserved. The expression of these preferences comes in letters to friends or to the authors themselves, and occasionally in articles. As can be seen from this list, her enjoyment was not as strictly constrained by her declared principles as might be feared. As always, she was more flexible in practice than in theory.

Edith Wharton's aesthetic, moral and social values are based on an ideal of order; her innate predisposition for order was confirmed and strengthened by her experience of life and art. The need for control, for rules and formulae based on tradition seemed to her to become more indispensable after the war when the principles of discipline, harmony, order, taste and proportion no longer underpinned assumptions in society or art. Her judgement continued to be founded on these principles as did her life and her craft. Inspiration ordered by reason; originality founded on tradition; feeling controlled by discipline; the balance between these opposing factors that she admired and sought to achieve and to express in her life and her non-fictional work is also seen to be basic to her theory of fiction.

CHAPTER TWO

Edith Wharton's Theory of Fiction

I: General Principles

For Edith Wharton the art of fiction lies in ordering and representing experience, real and imagined, through selection and form. Her ideals in fiction coincide with her ideals in life: traditional methods and forms, unity, proportion, moral certainty, harmony, are as basic to her principles in fiction as they are to her own life and to her concept of a healthy society and of beauty. Experience must, however, be transmuted in such a way that it creates an illusion of reality: 'verisimilitude is the truth of art' (*WF* 89) although one of the aims of art should be to order and give meaning to life: 'the eternal effort of art to complete what in life seems incoherent and fragmentary' (*WF* 107). One of the ways in which an author should do this is by conveying a sense of moral vision: 'every serious picture of life contains a thesis' ('Fiction and Criticism')[1].

Her rational mind – she describes herself in a letter to Daisy Chanler as 'the high priestess of the life of reason'[2] – was attracted to form, unity and clarity of purpose in art, but, although she expresses her ideals in general terms forcefully enough, her formulation of the specific means whereby the novelist can achieve these ends is vague and unsatisfactory. To some extent this is due to the nature of the task and she is aware of the difficulties; in *The Writing of Fiction*, her attempt to analyse the technique of story-telling, she points out that some readers might feel that 'in the quest for an intelligible working theory the gist of the matter has been missed. . . . It would appear that in the course of such enquiries the gist of the matter always does escape' (*WF* 118). She asks, therefore: 'Is it useless to try for a clear view of the meaning and method of one's art?' She obviously concludes that it is not, and expresses her belief in the importance of a coherent theory of the craft of fiction both for the novelist himself and for his successors:

The art of fiction, as now practised, is a recent one, and the arts of their earliest stages are seldom theorized on by those engaged in creating them; but as soon as they begin to take shape their practitioners, or at least those of the number who happen to think as well as to create, perforce begin to ask themselves questions. Some may not have Goethe's gift for formulating the answers, even to themselves; but these answers will eventually be discoverable in an added firmness of construction and appropriateness of expression. Other writers do consciously lay down rules, and in the search for new forms and more complex effects may even become the slaves of their too fascinating theories. These are the true pioneers, who are never destined to see their own work fulfilled, but build intellectual houses for the next generation to live in. . . . In the case of most novelists, such thought as they spare to the art, its range and limitations, far from sterilizing their talent will stimulate it by giving them a surer command of their means. (*WF* 116–18)

She declares that: 'If no art can be quite pent-up in the rules deduced from it, neither can it fully realize itself unless those who practise it attempt to take its measure and reason out its processes' (*WF* 119).

Her own attempt to reason out the processes of her art is expressed in *The Writing of Fiction*, published in 1924, about which she writes to W.C. Brownell of Scribner's: 'I really poured out my faith and reverence for my art';[3] in her autobiography, *A Backward Glance*, published in 1934; and in articles and reviews written mainly after 1927. (In her letters to friends, however, even those to Henry James, she rarely discusses her principles and aims in fiction although she frequently refers to the work in progress – sometimes using it as a social excuse: 'I am seeing hardly anyone at present, because I can't when I'm story-telling'[4] – or to reviews and opinions of recently published work.)

From these sources it can be seen that, although Edith Wharton asserts her belief in planning, in structure, in purpose and guiding principles in the art of fiction, her equally strong belief that living characters springing from particularized material and social conditions were the essence of the novel led her to distrust rigid formulae. As always, her classical ideas are tempered by her instinct and imagination. For example, in her 1920 article for the *Quarterly Review* 'Henry James in his Letters' she shows appreciation for James's attempts to formulate a theory of his art and defends his preoccupation with technique from what she describes as 'an inveterate tendency on the part of the Anglo-Saxon reader to regard "feeling" and "art" as antithetical'. She admires James for insisting that: 'every great novel must first of all be based on a profound sense of moral values ('importance of subject'), and then constructed with a classical unity and economy of means'.

Edith Wharton shares his belief in these two requisites for the novel:

> There is a sense in which the writing of fiction may be compared to the administering of a fortune. Economy and expenditure must each bear a part in it, but they should never degenerate into parsimony or waste. True economy consists in the drawing out of one's subject of every drop of significance it can give, true expenditure in devoting time, meditation and patient labour to the process of extraction and representation. (*WF* 57)

James describes her as a 'votary' of 'selection and intention'[5]. However close to James in these respects, she distances herself from him at the end of her article: 'Henry James, as his years advanced, and his technical ability became more brilliant, fell increasingly under the spell of his formula. From being a law almost unconsciously operative it became an inexorable convention'.

In the chapter on Henry James in her autobiography, published fourteen years after the 1920 article, she again distances herself from James's preoccupation with technique:

> I was naturally much interested in James's technical theories and experiments, though I thought and still think that he tended to sacrifice to them that spontaneity which is the life of fiction. Everything, in the latest novels, had to be fitted into a predestined design, and design, in his strict geometrical sense, is to me one of the least important things in fiction. (*BG* 190)

Earlier in *A Backward Glance* she pays tribute to Walter Berry's advice:

> 'Don't worry about how you're to go on. Just write down everything you feel like telling.' The advice freed me once for all from the incubus of an artificially pre-designed plan, and sent me rushing ahead with my tale, letting each incident create the next, and keeping in sight only the novelist's essential sign-post; the inner significance of the 'case' selected. (*BG* 115)

It is difficult to reconcile this view with her frequently expressed scorn for 'formlessness' and for 'anarchy in fiction' and with the following opinions, the second published in the same year as *A Backward Glance*:

> The fundamental difference between the amateur and the artist is the possession of the sense of technique: that is, in its broadest meaning, of the necessity of form. (*CF*)

Any lasting creative work must be based on some sort of constructive system. (*TMF*)

* * *

The important task is not to convict her of inconsistency, but to ask whether she found a balance between her belief in rules and formulae and her awareness of the necessity of allowing the creative imagination freedom. E.K. Brown feels that 'conscious art was the basis of all she wrote'.[6] Marilyn Lyde (1959) sees her as constantly trying in her fiction to find 'a way of harmonizing the dissecting intellect with the accepting soul'[7] – a phrase used by Edith Wharton in *A Backward Glance* (p. 159). Richard Poirier feels that 'the literary consequences of her confused feelings about impulse and order are apparent in the very best of her novels'[8]. She was fully aware of the problem of balancing what she calls inspiration with intellectual control; she resolved the problem in her fiction by showing her artist–hero, Vance Weston, learning to control his imagination and impulses through education and the gradual assimilation of traditional forms. In her own case, her notes and drafts for *Literature* – the unfinished and unpublished novel from which the Vance novels evolved – show that she planned and ordered carefully the material which sprang from her experience and imagination.

While succeeding in many of her novels in harmonizing inspiration and conscious art, she fails to formulate clearly a theory of the technique of fiction that balances her account of inspiration. She frequently expresses her belief in the need for a formula – 'each time the artist passes from dream to execution he will need to find the rules and formulas on the threshold' – but her attempt to expound one is confused. Nevertheless, while her ideas on method are imprecise, she does have clear-cut opinions on the aims of fiction.

Above all Edith Wharton thought that fiction should aim at producing an illusion of reality: 'Verisimilitude is the truth of art, and any convention which hinders the illusion is obviously in the wrong place' (*WF* 89). Much of her discussion of her own and others' work and of the technique of writing fiction is based on this premise. She concludes 'The Criticism of Fiction' (1914) by saying that the highest gift of the great novelists is that:

> Divining and life-evoking faculty which, whatever the method it resorts to for expression, is the very foundation of the novelist's art, and the result, not of this or that rule or theory, but of the intense and patient pondering on the depths of life itself.

She declares in a discussion of the ghost story, in which the problem of probability is at its greatest, that the author must contrive to create for the reader a sense of security: 'The greater the improbability to be overcome the more studied must be the approach, the more perfectly maintained the air of naturalness, the easy assumption that things are always likely to happen in that way' (WF 37). For, as 'a wise critic once said: "You may ask your reader to believe anything you can *make* him believe." ' To an author who defines the art of fiction as 'the creation of imaginary characters and the invention of their imaginary experiences' verisimilitude is primarily bound up with the creation of character. In 'Permanent Values in Fiction' (1934) she describes one of the two qualities which survive the verdict of time as: 'the creating of characters which so possess us with the sense of their reality that we talk of Anna Karenina, the Père Goriot, and Tess, as of real people whom we have known and lived with'.

Her belief that in the art of the novel it was 'the aliveness of the characters [which] seems the novel's one assurance of prolonged survival' is expressed in The Writing of Fiction, 'Tendencies in Modern Fiction' (1934), 'A Reconsideration of Proust' (1934), 'Permanent Values in Fiction' (1934), and earlier in 'The Vice of Reading' (1903) and 'Visibility in Fiction' (1929). Evidently this was a strongly held view. Edith Wharton considers characterization more frequently and more fully than any other aspect in her discussion of the art of fiction.

Although in her novels and in her travel books Edith Wharton stresses the importance of society's influence on the development and course of individual lives, she does not discuss in any detail the creation of the surroundings of fictional characters. Certainly the social setting was seen as vital to the illusion of reality both as background and as a controlling force in the lives of the characters. At the beginning of The Writing of Fiction, as part of her definition of modern fiction, she commends Balzac for being:

> the first not only to see his people, physically and morally, in their habit as they lived, with all their personal hobbies and infirmities, and make the reader see them, but to draw his dramatic action as much from the relation of his characters to their houses, streets, towns, professions, inherited opinions, as from their fortuitous contacts with each other. (WF 5)

Stendhal, too, is commended for differentiating his characters and for 'his insight into the springs of social action'. She continues:

> What was new in both Balzac and Stendhal was the fact of their viewing each character first of all as a product of particular material and social conditions, as being thus or thus because of the calling he pursued or the

house he lived in (Balzac), or the society he wanted to get into (Stendhal), or the acre of ground he coveted, or the powerful or fashionable personage he aped or envied (both Balzac and Stendhal). (*WF 7*)

For a novelist whose greatest strength is her skill in portraying society and manners with economy through telling detail – the cut of Ellen Olenska's dress at the opera, or Ann Eliza Bunner's 'double-dyed and triple-turned silk'[9] – it is disappointing that she does not discuss in any detail her own method in creating a convincing social background and in relating that background to the moral atmosphere surrounding an individual.

The second of the two qualities that Edith Wharton sees as criteria for judging the novel is the art of relating living characters 'to whatever general law made the novelist choose to tell their tale rather than another' (*PVF*). If a work is to be judged to have lasting value as art, it must contain moral significance. In theory she appears to see the moral vision of an author as belonging to the instinctive and imaginative side of the creation of fiction; in practice, as will be shown, the significance of a work is the outcome of careful selection of material. She implies that the need to find order in the 'welter of existence' is basic to the human condition and both reader and author 'instinctively' seek moral significance in the novel. As she had shown in her travel works, for her, anarchy in society – and architecture – signified moral anarchy, so in her criticism she sees moral order in the novel as a criterion of literary value.

Her unpublished article 'Fiction and Criticism'[10] contains her fullest discussion of this topic. She asserts that:

> The only really immoral book is that in which the writer has not felt keenly enough the relation of the little fraction of life he represents to the eternal truths, to bring his subject into relation with the latter.

A writer does not need to possess an admirable moral philosophy for 'the immoral writer is . . . the writer who lacks imagination'; she cites Balzac as 'lacking in the subtler ethical perceptions' and Stendhal as 'distinctly anti-social' but: 'By force of imagination, and by their magical divination of human motive, they produced, in books like *Père Goriot* and *Le Rouge et le Noir*, studies of life so penetrating as to be profoundly moral'.

The typescript of this article is emphasized by heavy underlining in the following manner:

> It cannot be too often repeated that every serious picture of life contains a thesis; what differentiates the literary artist from the professed moralist is not a radical contradiction of purpose, but the fact that the one instructs by his observation.

She quotes Maupassant's remark in his study of Flaubert: 'if a book teaches a lesson it must be in spite of its author, *by the mere force of the facts he narrates*'. She comments:

> This is an excellent definition of a good novel. The novelist ceases to be an artist the moment he bends his characters to the exigencies of a thesis; but he would equally cease to be one, should he draw the acts he describes without regard to their moral significance.

It is on these latter grounds that Edith Wharton makes her criticism of Proust in the final chapter in *The Writing of Fiction* although she does not allow her criticism to alter her view of Proust as 'a great creative artist': 'Where the qualities outweigh the defects the latter lose much of their importance, even when, as sometimes in Proust's case, they are defects in the moral sensibility, that tuning-fork of the novelist's art' (*WF* 171). His moral sensibility fails 'when he is unaware of the meanness of an act committed by one of his characters'. But these moments are mere lapses and she concludes by reiterating her view that the critic must 'linger only in reverent admiration of the great work achieved, the vast register covered'. In 'A Reconsideration of Proust' (1934) she declares that:

> The outward incidents he recorded, however brutal, and often repellent, concerned him only as manifestations of inner life. . . . In spite of Proust's individual antecedents his traditional world was still essentially a Christian and Catholic one; the moral and intellectual conflicts arising in such a society alone seemed to him to be worth recording.

She recalls in *A Backward Glance* that she had been encouraged by Henry James to tackle the subject of the society in which she had been brought up: 'Do New York! The first-hand account is precious.' The problem was how 'to extract from such a subject the typical human significance which is the story-teller's excuse for telling one story rather than another'. She felt that 'there are some subjects too shallow to yield anything to the most searching gaze'. She solved the problem by seeing that such a society 'can acquire dramatic significance only through what its frivolity destroys. Its tragic implication lies in its power of debasing people and ideals' (*WF* 207). *The House of Mirth* stands as justification of the wisdom of James's advice and of her interpretation of the subject matter. As she says in 'The Vice of Reading', published in 1903 while she was writing *The House of Mirth*: 'any serious portrayal of life must be judged not by the incidents it presents but by the author's sense of their significance'. At the same time, the incidents described illuminate the subject matter because the author has selected them for 'something that makes them crucial, some recognizable relation to a familiar social or moral standard, some explicit awareness of the eternal struggle between man's contending impulses' (*WF* 14).

Edith Wharton stresses the need for objectivity if the writer's moral vision is to be communicated to the reader: the writer must have the ability to 'stand away from the story to view it as a whole and relate it to its setting' (*WF* 78) and, as she says in 'The Great American Novel', 'to relate even trivial happenings to something greater'. The primary aims in a work of fiction, according to Edith Wharton, of creating living characters in a credible world and of giving those characters and their stories moral significance, can only be achieved by the artist striving to be objective and recognizing the necessity for a coherent technique.

II: Technique

Having declared in 'The Criticism of Fiction' that 'the fundamental difference between the amateur and the artist is the possession of the sense of technique, that is, in its broadest meaning, of the necessity of form', Edith Wharton defines form in *The Writing of Fiction* as 'the order, in time and importance, in which the narrative incidents are grouped' (*WF* 81). In order to achieve her stated aims of verisimilitude and moral purpose in the novel, she, in theory, at least, pursues classical methods of conscious selection and arrangement in the structure of the story and in the creation of character.

The idea of selection is basic to Edith Wharton's discussion of the art of fiction: choice of subject; of incidents to illuminate that subject; of where to begin and of length; of presentation to the reader – point of view, proportion of narrative to dialogue, style, time-scale; above all, choice of characters and of 'the conscious thoughts and deliberate actions which are the key to character, and to the author's reason for depicting that character'. She argues in 'The Criticism of Fiction', as she does in 'The Vice of Reading', that even those of her contemporaries most dedicated to formlessness cannot avoid selection:

> To imagine that form can ever be dispensed with is like saying that wine cannot be drunk without something to drink it from. The boundless gush of 'life', to be tasted and savoured, must be caught in some outstretched vessel of perception and to perceive is to limit and to choose . . . and once selection is exercised, why limit its uses, why not push it to the last point of its exquisite powers of pattern-making, and let it extract from raw life the last drop of figurative beauty?
>
> If, then, design is inevitable, the best art must be that in which it is most organic, most inherent in the soul of the subject.

Her opinion that aesthetic judgement as well as method should be based on an appreciation of selection and composition is returned to in *The Writing of Fiction* where she says that there is 'no way of estimating anything to which no standard of choice can be applied' (*WF* 17).

The Writing of Fiction, published in 1924, contains Edith Wharton's most serious attempt to express a theory about how a work of fiction, novel or short story, is or should be constructed. The book contains little reference to her own methods, which she reserves for an article 'Confessions of a Novelist' published in 1933 and later incorporated into her autobiography *A Backward Glance*: she draws her examples here from traditional novelists of the European past. In its form – the pattern of its chapters and the balanced prose – the work demonstrates her belief in 'Order the beauty even of Beauty is'.

Each of the first four chapters begins with historical background – with a side-swipe at those practitioners who disregard that background – continues with an attempt to classify types of novel or short story followed by a discussion of general principles; only then does she consider the process of writing a work of fiction. The fifth chapter shows how Marcel Proust exemplifies the principles she has laid down in the earlier part of the book, in particular that 'his strength is the strength of tradition'. Each chapter ends with a paragraph of vague supposition hardly appropriate in a book which she describes in her autobiography as an attempt to analyse the technique of fiction. For example, she ends the longest and most important chapter in the book, 'Constructing a Novel', thus:

> The novelist to whom this magic is not open has not even touched the borders of the art, and to its familiars the power of expression may seem innate. But it is not so. The creatures of that fourth-dimensional world are born as helpless as the human animal; and each time the artist passes from dream to execution he will need to find the rules and formulas on the threshold. (*WF* 121)

Rather as *Italian Villas* illustrates mainly the rational side to Edith Wharton, and *Italian Backgrounds* the imaginative, so do *The Writing of Fiction* and *A Backward Glance* exemplify, if more intentionally, these two sides respectively, while like the Italian books never remaining entirely either objective or subjective. If *The Writing of Fiction* does not succeed as an exposition of the technique of fiction, and often seems a pale reflection of Henry James's detailed explication of his art, it is of value to the student of Edith Wharton as an indication of her priorities and principles in writing fiction. Dating as it does from the last part of her life, it further illustrates the cast of her mind and that it is unchanged although crystallized since her first published work, *The Decoration of Houses*.

Having briefly outlined the origins and development of the novel and emphasized the importance of selection, form and tradition, Edith Wharton comes, in the first chapter of *The Writing of Fiction*, to 'the great, the central, matter of subject'. Although in her own case she declares in *A Backward Glance* that she 'never attached much importance to subject', here she lays down criteria for the novelist in selecting a subject. He must choose a subject appropriate to his talent and decide if the subject is suitable 'material for the imagination'[11]; is it a subject worth exploring and, if so, has the novelist power to extract to the full its value: 'A gold mine is worth nothing unless the owner has the machinery for extracting the ore'. Above all, a subject must contain moral significance:

> Any subject considered in itself must first of all respond in some way to that mysterious need of a judgement on life of which the most detached human intellect, provided it be a normal one, cannot, apparently, rid itself. . . . There seems to be no escape from this obligation. . . . In vain has it been attempted to set up a water-tight compartment between 'art' and 'morality'.

Once the subject has been selected, it must be allowed to gestate in the mind. One of her frequently reiterated maxims is that subjects should be 'brooded upon' before the question of form, narrative technique, characterization and style are addressed:

> If, when once drawn to a subject, he [i.e. the author] would let it grow slowly in his mind instead of hunting about for arbitrary combinations of circumstance, his tale would have the warm scent and flavour of a fruit ripened in the sun instead of the insipidity of one forced in a hot-house. (*WF* 57)

In her discussion of Proust in the final chapter of the book, she quotes Tyndall on 'great speculative minds': 'There is in the human intellect a power of expansion – I might almost call it a power of creation – which is brought into play by the simple brooding upon facts' and she comments: 'he might have added that this brooding is one of the most distinctive attributes of genius, is perhaps as near an approach as can be made to the definition of genius' (*WF* 166).

Earlier in *The Writing of Fiction* she declares that 'True originality consists not in a new manner but in a new vision' and that the mind in which the 'brooding' takes place should be capable of nourishing the subject 'with an accumulated wealth of knowledge and experience' (*WF* 18–19). Her thesis that the past nourishes the present and that only through knowledge and appreciation of tradition can a work of art be created is expressed even more imperatively when she writes of the art of fiction than when she deals with manners, society or the visual arts:

> The novelist of the present day is in danger of being caught in a vicious circle, for the insatiable demand for quick production tends to keep him in a state of perpetual immaturity, and the ready acceptance of his wares encourages him to think that no time need be wasted in studying the past history of his art, or in speculating on its principles. This conviction strengthens the belief that the so-called quality of 'originality' may be impaired by too long brooding on one's theme and too close a commerce with the past; but the whole history of that past – in every domain of it – disproves this by what survives, and shows that every subject to yield and to retain its full flavour, should be long carried in the mind, brooded upon, and fed with all the impressions and emotions which nourish its creator. (WF 18)

She demonstrates this thesis fictionally in the character of her writer–hero, Vance Weston.

The decision whether to present the material in the form of the short story or the novel needs to be made. According to Edith Wharton, the subject matter is inherently different, for 'every subject . . . must necessarily contain within itself its own dimensions' (WF 41) and the writer must learn to distinguish whether the subject is suitable for a short story or a novel. She mentions character, time-scale and point of view, and concludes:

> The chief technical difference between the short story and the novel may therefore be summed up by saying that situation is the main concern of the short story, character of the novel; and it follows that the effect produced by the short story depends almost entirely on its form, or presentation. (WF 48)

The shorter the story the more important is 'the precious instinct of selection' (WF 54) for 'it depends for its effect not only on the choice of what is kept when the superfluous has been jettisoned, but on the order in which these essentials are set forth'. (WF 54) The effect to be aimed at is, even more than in the novel, of 'presentness'. (WF 48) In discussing the construction of the novel, she declares that: 'The length of a novel, more surely even than any of its other qualities, needs to be determined by the subject' (WF 102). The novelist cannot decide in advance on the length of a work but must keep it in mind during its composition. The sense of proportion of their subjects is a characteristic of the great writers of fiction – by Edith Wharton's definition, Balzac, Tolstoy, Thackeray, George Eliot, Jane Austen. She cites *The Turn of the Screw* as an example of James's 'perfect sense of proportion', (*WF* 104) whereas in *The Sense of the Past* he was about to risk over-burdening his theme'. (*WF* 105) Flaubert too had 'the rare instinct of scale' (*WF* 106) and yet over-extends *L'Education Sentimentale*. The principle of proportion, so important to Edith Wharton's classical ideals in the visual arts, is as important in the art of the novel for it regulates disorder: 'Even the longest and most seemingly desultory novels of such writers as Balzac, Flaubert and Tolstoy follow a prescribed orbit; they are true to the eternal effort of art to complete what in life seems incoherent and fragmentary' (*WF* 107). She, indeed, uses an architectural image to describe the construction of a novel:

> Nietzsche said that it took genius 'to make an end' – that is, to give the touch of inevitableness to the conclusion of any work of art. In the art of fiction this is particularly true of the novel, that slowly built-up monument in which every stone has its particular weight and thrust to carry and of which the foundations must be laid with a view to the proportions of the highest tower. (*WF* 50)

As she says: 'The question of the length of a novel naturally leads to the considering of its end' (*WF* 108). She declares in the chapter 'Telling a Short Story': 'Obviously, as every subject contains its own dimensions, so is its conclusion *ab ovo*; and the failure to end a tale in accordance with its own deepest sense must deprive it of meaning' (*WF* 51). She adds little guidance towards the solution of this technical problem in the later chapter on 'Constructing the Novel':

> There is little to be said that has not already been implied by the way, since no conclusion can be right which is not latent in the first page. About no part of a novel should there be a clearer sense of inevitability than about its end; any hesitation, any failure to gather up all the threads, shows that the author has not let the subject mature in his mind. A novelist who does not know when his story is finished, but goes on string-ing episode to episode after it is all over, not only weakens the effect of the conclusion, but robs of significance all that has gone before. (*WF* 108)

The subject determines the ending as it does the length. As to the beginning, she feels that whereas in the novel the writer's first care should be for the ending, in the short story it should be 'to know how to make a beginning':

> The rule that the first page of a novel ought to contain the germ of the whole is even more applicable to the short story, because in the latter case the trajectory is so short that flash and sound nearly coincide. (*WF* 51)

She does, however, discuss the question of where to begin in considering the construction of the novel, and cites examples of different approaches, including Balzac's criticism of Stendhal's opening *La Chartreuse de Parme* with the Waterloo episode.

The question of appropriateness to the particular talent, of moral significance, of proportion and of the beginning and ending having been addressed, the author must consider how to present the material to the reader. Edith Wharton declares that: 'The mode of presentation to the reader, that central difficulty of the whole affair, must always be determined by the nature of the subject' (*WF* 72).

This statement concludes a discussion of the different types of novel, classified by her as 'manners, character (or psychology) and adventure' and typified respectively by *Vanity Fair*, *Madame Bovary*, and *Rob Roy* or *The Master of Ballantrae*. She suggests as subdivisions, the farcical novel of manners, the romance and the philosophical romance, and the 'hybrid' novel. Classification is crucial for the creator, for 'it means the choice of manner and an angle of vision'. As many subjects contain elements of several types of novel, one of the novelist's first cares is to select which method to use. She cites Henry James's *The Awkward Age* as an example of a novel where the manner of presentation, almost entirely through dialogue, is appropriate neither for the subject nor for the form of the novel: the subject in this case requires the elucidation that 'straight' narrative would have given it, and any subject that seems to be suited to being 'talked' demands the 'special artifices of the theatre'. The advantage of the novel form is that the author has the freedom to employ both narrative and dialogue, and she feels that: 'Narrative, with all its suppleness and variety . . . should furnish the substance of the novel; dialogue, that precious adjunct, should never be more than an adjunct' (*WF* 72).

She says in 'Confessions of a Novelist' that 'the situating of my tale, and its descriptive and narrative portions, I am conscious of conducting'. Yet neither in her articles nor in *The Writing of Fiction* does she discuss the composition of narrative, whereas in 'Confessions of a Novelist' she presents herself as 'merely the recording instrument' of dialogue.

She declares that 'the use of dialogue in fiction seems to be one of the few things about which a fairly definite rule may be laid down'. This rule is that dialogue should only be reserved for 'culminating moments'. The judicious use of dialogue as a contrast with narrative 'not only serves to emphasize the crises of the tale but to give it as a whole a greater effect of continuous development' (*WF* 75). Conversation should not be used as a means of carrying on the tale because the result will be improbability. As she says in a later chapter, 'Character and Situation':

The moment the novelist finds that his characters are talking not as they naturally would, but as the situation requires . . . his effect has been produced at the expense of reality. . . . His characters must talk as they would in reality, and yet everything not relevant to his tale must be eliminated. The secret of success lies in selection. (*WF* 140–2)

Dialogue must, above all, seem convincingly real but this is achieved through careful selection; yet in 'Confessions of a Novelist' she says:

My hand never hesitates because my mind has not to choose, but only to set down what these stupid or intelligent, lethargic or passionate people say to each other in a language and with arguments, that appear to be all their own.

But she goes on to repeat the point she made in *The Writing of Fiction* that it is 'only significant passages of their talk [that] should be recorded in high relief against the narrative'.

Edith Wharton's comments on the use of dialogue contain, amongst the repetitions, a useful precept, that it should be employed sparingly and significantly at key moments with verisimilitude as the guiding principle. Again, the classical tenet of proportion and the importance of conscious selection underlie her theory. In practice, her use of dialogue was seen as achieving the objectives she set out: Henry James, in his article for *The Times Literary Supplement* on 'The Younger Generation' (which became 'The New Novel') in April 1914 – to which Edith Wharton's 'Criticism of Fiction' was a reply – says of *The Custom of the Country* and 'Mrs Wharton's other fictions': 'the whole series' offers 'an example of dialogue flowering and not weeding, illustrational and not itself starved of illustration, or starved of referability and association'.

The principles of selection and careful ordering also underlie her idea of 'illuminating incidents': that is, scenes in a novel which make clear to the reader the significance of that particular situation, and which also elucidate themes and characters in the work as a whole. These incidents are 'the best means of giving presentness, immediacy, to [the] tale' (*WF* 112). Although Edith Wharton employs romantic language in attempting to explain her idea – 'illuminating incidents are the magic casements of fiction' – she demonstrates clearly what she means through examples. The most telling of these are from Flaubert's *L'Education Sentimentale* when Moreau and Mme Arnoud meet again after many years and the lamp lights up her white hair; from James's *The Golden Bowl* when Maggie watches through the window from the terrace her husband, her father and his wife playing bridge inside; and where in Stendhal's *Le Rouge et le Noir* Julian first takes Mme Reynal's hand. These examples come from different points in the respective works, the end, the middle and the beginning, and illustrate how a scene can make clear what has gone before and what is coming, and also reveal character and situation. 'Threads of significance are gathered up into each one' as Edith Wharton puts it. She feels that 'illuminating incidents' are:

> The most personal element in any narrative, the author's most direct contribution; and nothing gives such immediate proof of the quality of his imagination – and therefore of the richness of his temperament – as his choice of such episodes. (WF 109)

The selection of incidents is important but it is not everything: there is also the manner of presenting these significant scenes where every word should 'tell'. The 'particular manner adapted to each scene' leads on to a consideration of the style of the whole work: 'As every tale contains its own dimension, so it implies its own manner, the particular shade of style most fitted to convey its full meaning' (WF 114). Unfortunately, Edith Wharton does not develop her ideas on style, but launches into a diatribe against 'indolent readers and reviewers' who prefer an author 'to give only what he has given before' rather than vary his manner of writing.

In the introductory chapter to *The Writing of Fiction*, she defines style as:

> The way in which they [i.e. the incidents] are presented, not only in the narrower sense of language, but also, and rather, as they are grasped and coloured by their medium, the narrator's mind, and given back in his words. (WF 24)

The distinction between language and the narrator's words is hard to understand. Edith Wharton appears to mean that there is some way in which language is objectively arrived at – 'the narrower sense' – and another in which it is subjectively chosen. It is not that she is making a distinction between conscious and unconscious art, for she continues:

> It is the quality of the medium [i.e. the narrator's mind] which gives these incidents their quality; style, in this sense, is the most personal ingredient in the combination of things out of which any work of art is made. Words are the exterior symbols of thought, and it is only by their exact use that the writer can keep on his subject the close and patient hold which 'fishes the murex up' and steeps his creation in unfading colours. (WF 24)

Apart from the trivial point that she also considers the choice of 'illuminating incidents' as the most personal element, she appears to be confusing or combining the idea that subject matter requires appropriate and particular language with the idea that every *writer* has, or should have, an individual and characteristic way of interpreting and expressing his material. The author must seek 'le mot juste' to express the material of his imagination in a distinctive way. She continues her short but longest discussion of style characteristically: 'Style in this definition is discipline.' To sum up this view she quotes Proust's analysis in *A l'Ombre de Jeunes Filles en Fleurs* of the art of his character the novelist Bergotte:

> The severity of his taste, his unwillingness to write anything of which he could not say, in his favourite phrase: *C'est doux* (harmonious, delicious), this determination, which caused him to spend so many seemingly fruitless years in the previous 'carving' of trifles, was in reality the secret of his strength; for habit makes the style of the writer as it makes the character of the man. (*WF* 25)

In her own case, she felt that it was through a similar devotion, through 'the discipline of the daily task, that inscrutable "inspiration of the writing table" ', that she turned from an amateur into a professional writer; this view that discipline and dedication are essential to the writer concurs with her opinions on creating harmony and proportion in society and domestic life.

Edith Wharton does not in *The Writing of Fiction* or elsewhere analyse in any detail the elements of style. In *A Backward Glance* she tells of her gratitude to Walter Berry for, amongst much else, his continued criticism of her work: 'With each book he exacted a higher standard in economy of expression, in purity of language, in the avoidance of the hackneyed and the previous.' Apart from a passing reference in 'Criticism of Fiction', the only other significant comment on style comes in her review of Leslie Stephen's *George Eliot* written in May 1902 for Bookman in which she says of George Eliot as an author what Faust said of himself as a man – and might well be said of Edith Wharton as an author and a woman: '*Zwei Seelen wohnen, ach, in meine Brust*' [Two spirits, alas, dwell in my breast]. Edith Wharton feels that George Eliot's style is 'rapid and varied in dialogue' and lacks both these qualities in narrative 'yet in character-drawing it is far less heavy and diffuse than in passages of "reflection" '. She feels that 'the observer of life is a better writer than a moralist'. With Edith Wharton, it might be said that the observer of life that is seen in her autobiography and fiction is a better writer than the critic and authority, who is often either shrill and didactic or unsubstantial.

Possibly it is because Edith Wharton regards the selection of 'illuminating incidents' and the manner of presenting those incidents as highly individual that she does not, or cannot, discuss the technical

problems. Her central technical concerns with the mode of presentation in the novel and short story focus on point of view and the
effect of the passage of time. These two 'unities' she describes as 'the
old traditional one of time, and the other, more modern and complex
which requires that any rapidly enacted episode shall be seen through
only one pair of eyes' (WF 43). In the short story the effect sought is
of 'compactness and instantaneity', and a single reflecting consciousness gives the story unity and plausibility. In the novel, where the
'longer passage of time and more crowded field of vision' requires
more than one point of view if the illusion of reality is to be
preserved, Edith Wharton felt that it was best 'to let the tale work
itself out from not more than two (or at the most three) angles of
vision' (WF 87) and to shift from one to the other as seldom
as possible.

'The story-teller's first care, after the choice of subject, is to decide
to which of his characters the episode in question happened' (WF 87).
She commends Henry James for being the first novelist, not, she
assumes, to consider what point of view to employ, but to formulate
the principle. The principles she lays down for a reflecting consciousness are, firstly, Henry James's that the character chosen should be
capable of taking 'the widest possible view of the situation', and
secondly, that the character should never be allowed to record
anything 'not naturally within his register'. In the novel, in order to
preserve a 'unity of impression' while employing more than one angle
of vision, the author must choose as reflectors people who, as well as
meeting these criteria, are either in 'close mental and moral relation to
each other', or who are capable of understanding each other's part in
the story.

If the selection of reflecting consciousness is hard, determining
when to change from one to another is still harder:

> The only possible rule seems to be that when things happen which the
> first reflector cannot, with any show of probability, be aware of, or is
> incapable of reacting to, even if aware, then another, or adjoining,
> consciousness takes up the tale. (WF 88)

But, she declares, this formula will 'act of itself' if the novelist has
allowed his subject to 'ripen in his mind' sufficiently. When a
discussion of technique is becoming difficult Edith Wharton tends to
retreat into romantic language and metaphors. Although she is elusive
when it comes to details of her craft, she is always positive in her
precepts: 'Verisimilitude is the truth of art, and any convention which
hinders the illusion is obviously in the wrong place.' In particular, she
derides some novelists for violating this axiom with 'the slovenly

habit of tumbling in and out of their characters' minds, and then suddenly drawing back to scrutinize them from the outside' (*WF* 89). While she commends Henry James for his skill in effecting the transition from one consciousness to another in *The Wings of the Dove*, she criticizes him for his invention of an 'insufferable and incredible' couple, the Assinghams, in *The Golden Bowl* purely as devices to reveal details of the situation and condemns the 'utter improbability' of their behaviour.

Consistent handling of point of view gives the work form and unity and is essential for the creation of verisimilitude. Even the landscape and setting should only be described in terms of what 'the intelligence concerned would have noticed' and in the appropriate style. Edith Wharton cites two examples from Thomas Hardy's novels, one of the observance of this rule and the other of the neglect. For the former, she points to the description of Egdon Heath as Eustacia Vye looks at it from Rainbarrow; for the latter, when he gives a 'painfully detailed description' of the countryside through which Tess 'unseeing, wretched, and incapable at any time of noting such particularities as it has amused her creator to set down flies blindly to her doom' (*WF* 85–6).

If Edith Wharton's discussion of point of view is scanty, she does, at least, focus on two important questions: choice of the angle of vision from which the situation is seen and consistency in handling one or more centres of consciousness. When it comes to her discussion of how the passage of time is conveyed in fiction, she is less precise and even less comprehensive. She promises, in the second chapter of *The Writing of Fiction*, to explore in the third chapter 'that central mystery – of which Tolstoy was perhaps the one complete master – the art of creating in the reader's mind this sense of passing time' but her use of the word 'mystery' prefigures the evasiveness of her approach to the second of 'the two central difficulties of the novel'. Apart from her recommendation that dialogue in contrast with narrative 'enhances that sense of the passage of time for the producing of which the writer has to depend on his intervening narration', her only advice is to 'go slowly' and 'to keep down the tone of the narrative, to be as colourless and quiet as life often is in the intervals between high moments'. The ability to create the effect of the gradual passage of time so that the characters seem to grow older and wiser naturally and convincingly is 'the great mystery of the art of fiction'; 'the secret seems incommunicable'. She recommends patience, meditation and concentration – which she characteristically alleges to be 'quiet habits of mind now so little practised, so seldom inculcated' (*WF* 96) – to which she adds the essential ingredient, genius. These remarks represent her promised exploration of the techniques for conveying the passage of time.

Characterization is the most important aspect of the novel to Edith Wharton: as has been said, she devotes more space to discussing it than to any other feature and much of her discussion of other aspects revolves around it. Dialogue, illuminating incidents, point of view, time, are all seen primarily as contributing factors in the creation of credible characters. Form itself should be subordinate to characters: to impose a structure on them, rather than to allow the form of the tale to 'grow out of what they are', destroys the illusion that they are living people, and 'the test of the novel is that the people should be ALIVE' (*WF* 48). Yet, as well as asserting that the creation of characters is the most important aspect of the art of the novel she attempts more seriously than in her discussion of other techniques to show how this is achieved. (In the short story where 'situation is the main concern', though characters must be 'a little more than puppets' they may be 'a little less than individual human beings'.)

Although Edith Wharton strives to analyse the techniques used by novelists who successfully created living creatures, as in all her discussion of technique she retreats into oracular utterances. In 'Visibility in Fiction', written for the *Yale Review* and her most sustained attempt 'to probe this mystery of visibility', she writes of a 'mysterious faculty', 'mysterious element' and 'magic' during her exploration, and in her conclusion refers to 'some secret intuition' possessed by those authors who were the 'greatest life-givers'. If she does not succeed in the course of the article in detecting what the 'trick' is, she does offer in her choice of example and in her reasons for her choice some useful comments on the creation of visible characters. Having show by reference to successful characters from novels of all categories the truth of her proposition that 'the aliveness of the characters seems the novel's one assurance of prolonged survival', Edith Wharton tries to 'detect what makes for visibility'. Dicken's characters, while indisputably visible, 'live only in their story', Tolstoy's characters in *War and Peace* 'live as we live, in time and space'. The trick of depicting characters by identifying them by idiosyncrasies of word, gesture or conduct 'seldom results in complete visibility': it merely suggests it. At this point where she seems about to go on to reveal the secret of creating visible characters, she avoids being specific:

> Sometimes one is inclined to think that visibility is achieved simply by the author's own intense power of seeing his characters in their habit as they lived, and by his ability to reproduce the color of his vision in words.

But she does make an interesting point – characteristically through example – that, although 'vivid picturing' makes the characters physically visible, some of the most alive characters in literature possess few if any physical characteristics:

> Do we any of us really know what Mrs. Proudie looked like, or Archdeacon Grantley? or even the great Lady Glencora? Who ever actually *saw* a Dostoevsky or a Turgenev character with the eyes of the flesh? And as for Jane Austen's, one almost wonders if she ever saw them bodily herself, so little do their physical peculiarities seem to concern her.

If lavish description is not the secret of making characters come alive – she cites George Meredith's characters as failures despite 'the richest of epithets and epigrams' – she asks: 'How, then, is the magic wrought?'

She answers the question she has reached through reasoning by retreating into romantic surmise:

> It is a truism to say that it all depends on a measure of the novelist's genius. Of course; but what is the particular faculty of genius that produces, by means so different, the identical quality of *quietness*; almost to that slow taking of pains which was once thought the fundamental attribute of genius. Certainly the great novelists, even those (chiefly those) who packed their pages with immortality while the printer's devil waited in the passage, seem never to have written in a hurry. There were days when, obviously, they had no time to correct their grammar or make sure of their syntax; hardly ever a day when they could not let their characters ripen and round themselves under the sunlight of a steady contemplation. It must be, then, surely, this mysterious faculty, something so intimate and compelling, so much like a natural process, that outward accidents, the hurry and worry of the surface, can never check, can seldom even distort it. Once called into life the beings thus created continue their dumb germination in the most tormented mind, if the mind be a great novelist's; and by the time they are born into the book which is their world they are such well constituted organisms that they live on in our world after theirs has ended.

This passage is characteristic of Edith Wharton's approach to the technique of fiction; the 'high priestess of the life of reason' is clearly a romantic in her concept of 'genius' and she falls back on this concept when she finds that she is unable to answer the questions she has posed. When she discusses the characters in her novels in *A Backward Glance* she does so entirely in terms of 'inspiration' as will be seen in the following chapter. 'Visibility in Fiction' raises two further problems in creating living characters: that of introducing them initially in a novel with many characters in such a way that they are immediately distinguishable, and that of sustaining visibility, which is harder than evoking it briefly. She offers three practical suggestions towards solving the first problem: avoid overcrowding the opening pages, allow the reader time to get used to one character before introducing another, and concentrate on the main characters. (She points out how successfully Tolstoy defies these elementary principles in *Resurrection*.) She is less specific in her answer to the second problem: she points to Balzac, Jane Austen, Thackeray, Tolstoy and Proust 'perhaps as an only fifth' as being the only novelists who 'could give this intense and unfailing visibility to their central characters as well as to the episodical figures of the periphery', which implies, as she rightly says, that the problem is insoluble:

> Yet we may still conjecture that a common denominator is, after all, to be found in the patient intensity of attention which these great novelists concentrated on each of their imagined characters, in their intimate sense of the reality of what they described, and in some secret intuition that the barrier between themselves and their creatures was somehow thinner than the pages of a book.

In *The Writing of Fiction* Edith Wharton shows the novel as progressing toward the point where 'the "action" of the novel was transferred from the street to the soul' and then when the characters became 'breathing and recognizable human beings'. Balzac and Stendhal were the first to see each character 'as a product of particular material and social conditions' and also to be aware that 'the bounds of personality are not reproducible by a sharp black line, but that each of us flows imperceptibly into adjacent people and things' (*WF* 7). But those authors who have taken the idea of portraying the inner life of characters and the idea of the fluidity of personality to produce the stream of consciousness method are castigated for two reasons: first because, despite the claim of its practitioners, it is not original, being related to the method used by the early French realists, *tranche de vie*, and having been used by the greatest novelists of the past as part of the picture of the whole character; second, because, contrary to belief, it does not create an illusion of reality, for 'in the world of normal men life is conducted, at least in its decisive moments, on fairly coherent and selective lines' (*WF* 13). And the novel's concern is with the decisive moments in a character's life rather than with recording every impression: 'The art of rendering life in fiction can never, in the last analysis, be anything, or need be anything, but the disengaging of crucial moments from the welter of existence' (*WF* 14).

Verisimilitude in characterization requires careful selection. In the chapter 'Character and Situation', Edith Wharton adds that even those who employ the stream of consciousness method cannot avoid being selective: 'the biggest bag is only, in the last resort, selection' (*TMF*). She warns that, having discarded the framework of the arbitrary plot in favour of the study of character, authors should not then reject all 'action necessary to illustrate characters' and give themselves over to the 'tedious' stream of consciousness method, or exaggerate trivial incidents to illustrate trivial lives.

The secret of characterization is not copying from life, as she says in *A Backward Glance*: 'Real people transported into a work of the imagination would instantly cease to be real; only those born of the creator's brain can give the least illusion of reality' (*BG* 210). What, then, is the secret? The techniques for creating vivid characters, as expressed in *The Writing of Fiction*, are to make them appear to control their own destinies, to think of characters first and 'their predicament only as the outcome of what they are', to allow them to speak as 'they naturally would' rather than as mouthpieces for their creator, to develop the tale through episodes all of which illustrate the characters or their social setting, to include nothing that is not relevant to the characters, to be objective about them.

She stresses the importance of objectivity at the end of her chapter on 'Constructing the Novel', and, although her exposition is of little practical value, it contains the kernel of her views on art – that 'Transmutation is the first principle of art', whether from life into art or, as she is saying in this extract, from the imagination into art:

> To the artist his world is as solidly real as the world of experience, or even more so, but in a way entirely different; it is a world to and from which he passes without any sense of effort, but always *with an uninterrupted awareness* of the passing. In this world are begotten and born the creatures of his imagination, more living to him than his own flesh-and-blood, but whom he never thinks of as living, in the reader's simplifying sense. Unless he keeps his hold on this dual character of their being, visionary to him, and to the reader real, he will be the slave of his characters and not their master. . . . Once projected by his fancy they are living beings who live their own lives; but their world is the one consciously imposed on them by their creator. Only by means of this objectivity of the artist can his characters lives in art. (*WF* 120)

Lack of objectivity is one reason why, according to Edith Wharton, central characters tend to be the least real because they are often, 'without the author's being aware of it, the standard-bearers of his convictions or the expression of his own secret inclinations' (*WF* 133). Not only are the leading figures often too much part of the author to be portrayed objectively, but because the story is about them, it may shape them rather than the other way round.

Her discussion in *The Writing of Fiction* of characterization is concerned with aims and pitfalls, and it also contains advice on how to keep characters as the focal point of the novel. Although she ends the chapter 'Constructing a Novel', with the assertion that the artist needs 'rules and formulas' to transmute the characters of his imagination into the people of his novel, she never discloses any such regulations. Indeed, she says about introducing a large cast of characters slowly or all at once that: 'There is no fixed rule about this, or about any other method; each, in the art of fiction, to justify itself has only to succeed' (*WF* 100). Even when she is dealing with character, to her the *raison d'être* of the novel, she is confused not only about the nature of the techniques used to achieve verisimilitude, but also about the possibility – or even the virtues of – producing a clear-cut theory. In the later articles she does not add to or clarify her ideas either on characterization or on any other aspect of the novel.

Edith Wharton has little difficulty in formulating clear principles and methods for the decoration of houses, for laying out a garden, or for civilized living; yet, while she holds to the same principles, she has difficulty in being specific about methods of construction and presentation in the art of fiction. She does not reconcile her desire for clear-cut rules for creating a work of fiction with her instinct that there can be few for such a fluid art form. As a result she contradicts herself, and does so not in later work but within *The Writing of Fiction*. She is not even consistent about what she considers to be the 'central difficulty' or 'the central mystery'.

Albeit confused and repetitious, Edith Wharton's attempt to express a theory of fiction shows how seriously she regarded fiction as an art; and, while not successful as objective analyses of the craft, *The Writing of Fiction* and the critical articles expose some central problems and are enlivened by well-chosen examples of techniques mentioned. But the greatest value lies in what this body of work reveals about Edith Wharton's precepts and priorities as a writer of fiction. She consciously wants order in the art of fiction based on traditional methods and on the classical values of proportion, harmony and moral certainty achieved through selection and planning. But, equally, she has an impulse towards romantic values and the freedom of the imagination, away from conscious design and towards spontaneity.

CHAPTER THREE

Inspiration and Imagination

For Edith Wharton the theory of fiction cannot be isolated from the individual author with his or her unique qualities; method is dependent on 'magic'. Alongside her belief in classical principles lies a romantic concept of inspiration and imagination. As has been seen, in *The Writing of Fiction* she often retreats from objective analysis of technique into references to the inaccessible inner world of the artist:

> The gist of the matter always escapes, since it nests, the elusive bright-winged thing, in that mysterious fourth-dimensional world which is the artist's inmost sanctuary and on the threshold of which enquiry must perforce halt. (*WF* 119)

In *A Backward Glance* she attempts to describe her own inspiration and imagination. In her unpublished novel, *Literature*, and the two published works which grew out of it, *Hudson River Bracketed* and *The Gods Arrive*, she dramatizes the inner creative process. She presents inspiration as a mystical, inexplicable force welling up from depths within the writer, and imagination as a response to external stimuli, seizing on 'snatches, glimpses – the seeds of things' and transforming them into 'the stuff of a book'. She explores this dual source of creativity in greater depth in the novels than she does in her autobiography, by showing the thought processes of the artist/hero and by symbol placed in that central consciousness and in the narrative outside it.

In her autobiography she declares that she has tried many times to discover '*how it is all done*, and exactly what happens at that "fine point of the soul" where the creative act, like the mystic's union with the Unknowable, really seems to take place' (*BG* 121). She devotes a chapter entitled 'The Secret Garden'[1] to an exploration of what 'for want of a simpler term, one must call by the old bardic name of inspiration' (*BG* 199). This was intended to complement what she saw as her analysis of technique in *The Writing of Fiction* and to complete an analysis of the two parts of 'the story-telling process'. She talks of the 'teeming visions' of her inner world and declares that what she means to try for is

> the observation of that strange moment when the vaguely adumbrated characters whose adventures one is preparing to record are suddenly *there*, themselves, in the flesh, in possession of one, and in command of one's voice and hand. It is there that the central mystery lies, and perhaps it is as impossible to fix in words as that other mystery of what happens in the brain at the precise moment when one falls over the edge of consciousness into sleep. (*BG* 198)

She presents herself as a passive vessel[2] awaiting the arrival of inspiration: 'it is sometimes the situation, the "case", which first presents itself, and sometimes the characters who appear, asking to be fitted into a situation'. After these initial appearances, either characters 'creep up and wriggle into it' (the situation) or 'the character draws nearer, and seems to become aware of me, and to feel the shy but desperate need to unfold his or her tale' (*BG* 200). Characters always, she asserts, arrive complete with their names or sometimes, 'a still more spectral element' (*BG* 202), names without characters. She is conscious of placing the tale in a particular setting and of conducting its descriptive and narrative passages but, she declares, she is 'merely a recording instrument' when it comes to dialogue and the 'subsidiary action' of the characters.

The image of the secret garden which she uses as the title for the chapter and in which she says she wants to try 'to depict the growth and unfolding . . . from the seed to the shrub-top' is characteristic of Edith Wharton and conveys both the idea of inspiration as spontaneous and mysterious and the idea of cultivation, of conscious craft. The seeds which fall into Edith Wharton's garden are not permitted to run wild but are nurtured, pruned and brought to fruition in fertile and carefully prepared soil. The image she uses for Vance Weston's inconstant inspiration in *The Gods Arrive* similarly gives an impression of magic and skill: 'Yet there were days when a grain of mustard seed, like an Indian conjuror's tree, would suddenly shoot up and scale the sky' (*GA* 172). But the emphasis in the first section of 'The Secret Garden' is on the mystical and mysterious nature of inspiration, either gushing up from inner, unconscious sources or gradually appearing in the conscious mind: she deals, she says, with 'the question of how some of my own novels happened to me, how each little volcanic island shot up from the unknown depths, or each coral-atoll slowly built itself' (*BG* 200).[3]

Again the artist's role appears to be passive, but once the initial ideas, mainly concerned with the characters, have arrived, his or her objective reasoning powers are applied. She ends the section: 'I can only say that the process, though it takes place in some secret garden on the sheer edge of consciousness, is always illuminated by the full light of my critical attention' (*BG 205*). She had expressed the same idea in *The Writing of Fiction*:

> Many people asume that the artist receives, at the outset of his career, the mysterious sealed orders known as 'Inspiration', and has only to let the sovereign impulse carry him where it will. Inspiration does indeed come at the outset to every creator, but it comes most often as an infant, helpless, stumbling, inarticulate, to be taught and guided. (*WF* 20)

If the language Edith Wharton uses to describe inspiration in her autobiography – 'mystery', 'soul', 'vision' – gives the impression that she sees the source of creativity as mysterious and unknowable – and this impression is reinforced in her fiction – it is balanced by the importance she places on the qualities innate in the writer. She stresses that in her own case from earliest childhood she possessed an imagination which responded eagerly to direct experience and which fed an instinct for words. Looking back on her childhood, she pictures that:

> My imagination lay there, coiled and sleeping, a mute hibernating creature, and at the least touch of common things – flowers, animals, words, especially the sound of words, apart from their meaning – it already stirred in its sleep, and then sank back into its own rich dream. (*BG* 4)

Her active imagination produced throughout her life an inner world 'as intense and with as great an appearance of reality' as the world outside. This intense inner life and fascination with words she relates to an impulse to create:

> The imagining of tales. . . . had gone on in me since my first conscious moments; I cannot remember the time when I did not want to 'make-up' stories. . . . Oddly enough, I had no desire to write my stories down (even had I known how to write, and I couldn't yet form a letter); but from the first I had to have a book in my hand to 'make-up' with. . . . At any moment the impulse might seize me; and then, if the book was in reach, I had only to walk the floor, turning the pages as I walked, to be swept off full sail on the sea of dreams. . . . Parents and nurses, peeping at me through the cracks of doors (I always had to be alone to 'make-up'), noticed that I often held the pages upside down, but that I never failed to turn the pages. (*BG* 33–4)

Neither the world of the imagination nor the instinct to create stories from it ever left her, as she claims at the end of the first section of 'The Secret Garden':

> My two lives, divided between these equally real yet totally unrelated worlds, have gone on thus, side by side, equally absorbing, but wholly isolated from each other, ever since in my infancy I 'read stories' aloud to myself out of Washington Irving's 'Alhambra', which I generally held upside down. (*BG* 205)

In the unfinished novel *Literature*, the early version of her *Künstler-roman*, she dramatizes this habit of 'making up' as she does the early interest in words: the 'two lives' of the writer figures as a theme in *Hudson River Bracketed* and *The Gods Arrive*.

Despite her claim at the beginning of 'The Secret Garden' that it will contain an exploration of the 'central mystery', she discusses the inner sources of her art only briefly and in the vaguest terms. She asserts that she 'can think of nothing corresponding to these self-confessions in the world of letters, or at any rate of fiction' the nearest being Henry James's Prefaces which she discounts on the grounds that they are mainly analyses of technique; even his appeal to his Genius is an invocation rather than 'an objective notation of her descent into his soul' (*BG* 198). The implication is that she will at least attempt such a notation, yet she devotes the greater part of the chapter to demonstrating how she developed from an amateur to a professional writer and includes two digresssions, one scornfully deriding the demands of the critics for fiction concerned only with 'the man with the dinner pail', and the other, equally scornful, refuting the 'exasperating' accusations by the public of putting 'real' people into novels.

She uses three novels to trace her progress from her first attempts at authorship to professional status – *The Valley of Decision*, *The House of Mirth* and *Ethan Frome*. Her first novel she dismisses as 'only a romantic chronicle' and she doubted at the time whether she 'should ever have enough constructive power to achieve anything beyond isolated character studies, or the stringing together of picturesque episodes' (*BG* 205). But her instinct as a story-teller – and her imagination always 'swarmed with subjects' – led her to consider how to use 'the material closest to hand', that is , New York. The problem was how to extract human significance from a superficial, pleasure-seeking society: once she had decided that 'its tragic implication lies in its power of debasing people and ideals' the novel's climax was clear but the distractions of friends and travel, reading and gardening made progress slow. It was because Scribner's magazine asked to serialize the novel at short notice that she was bent to 'the discipline of the daily task, that inscrutable "inspiration of the writing table" ' and was forcibly 'turned from the drifting amateur into a professional'. Even more important, she says, was

> the effect on my imagination of systematic daily effort. I was really like Saul the son of Kish, who went out to find an ass, and came back with a kingdom: the kingdom of mastery over my tools. (*BG* 209)

Nevertheless, it was not until *Ethan Frome* that she felt 'the artisan's full control of his implements' and since

> that day until now I have always felt that I had my material fairly well in hand, though so often, alas, I am conscious that the strange beings who have commissioned me to tell their story are not satisfied with the portraits I have drawn of them. (*BG* 209)

The lack of detail Edith Wharton gives about either the initiating force or the development of the novels, about either her inspiration or her creative imagination, whose function she says in *The Writing of Fiction* is to convert intellectual and moral experience into the material of art, means that the pictures of conscious and unconscious processes of her story-telling is blurred. By comparison James's Prefaces, which failed, in Edith Wharton's view, to explore the 'central mystery', contain, as well as exposition of technique, the 'private history' of a *donnée*, its growth and development, the dramatization and working out of the moral significance, and the gradual emergence of the characters. From such detail a clear picture of the way in which his imagination worked emerges. In the case of Edith Wharton it is only through examination of notes and drafts for a novel (Chapter Four) that a substantial picture of the creative process appears; it is in her fiction about the writer that her ideas on inspiration and imagination are developed.

* * *

In *Hudson River Bracketed* and *The Gods Arrive* Edith Wharton explores the sources of creativity in the artist: she shows the writer/hero's need to 'plumb the depths' within himself and relate those mystical depths to universal forces as well as his need to feed his imagination with experience of the outside world and knowledge of the accumulated wisdom of the past. Vance Weston, her hero, not only embodies her views on inspiration and imagination but is also a standard-bearer for her convictions about tradition, continuity, order, discipline and education.

The close relationship between Edith Wharton and Vance Weston is clear: to Vance, subjects: 'abounded – swarmed like bees, hummed in his ears like mosquitoes. There were times when he could hardly see the real world for his crowding visions of it' (*HRB* 199). Vance reflects on a new novel to be called *Magic*,[4] watching the arrival of his characters:

> The curtain went up on his inner stage – one by one the characters came on – first faintly outlined, then more clearly, at last in full illumination. The outer world vanished. . . . Of all the myriad world nothing was left but this tiny centre of concentrated activity, in which creatures born without his will lived out their complicated and passionate lives. . . . They were there, they were real, they were the sole reality, and he who was the condition of their existence was yet apart from them, and empowered to be their chronicler. (*HRB* 373–4)

The language she uses to describe Vance's inspiration echoes that she uses to describe her own: 'divine', 'dream', 'vision', 'soul', 'spirit', 'mysterious', 'mystical'. Throughout the novels romantic language and images recur. Near the beginning of *Hudson River Bracketed* Vance, newly arrived in the East from the Midwest, is revealed as possessing the soul of the artist:

> There were times when his own soul was like a forest, full of shadows and murmurs – *arcane, aloof* – a place to lose one's way in, a place fearsome, almost, to be alone in. . . . He often felt as if his own soul where a stranger inside of him, a stranger speaking a language he had never learned, or had forgotten. (*HRB* 39)

Later, in the library of 'The Willows', the house typifying the architectural style designated Hudson River Bracketed and symbolizing the past to Vance, he

> continued to sit motionless, letting the secret forces move within him. Whenever he could surrender to his creative fervour it always ended by carrying him to the mysterious point where effort ceased, and he seemed just to have to hold his breath and watch. (*HRB* 243)

As he writes his novel while his wife lies dying in the next room:

> He knew, as never before, the rapture of great comet flights of thought across the heaven of human conjecture, and the bracing contact of subjects minutely studied, without so much as a glance beyond their borders. Now and then he would stop and let his visions sweep him

away; then he would return with renewed fervour to the minute scrutiny of his imaginary characters. There was something supernatural and compulsory in this strange alternation between creating and dreaming. (*HRB* 392)

Hudson River Bracketed is concerned with the innate qualities of the writer, with his inspiration and imagination, and with the way in which he learns to use his talents; *The Gods Arrive* focuses on the way in which a writer who has come to terms with technique learns to keep his internal world in balance with his external experiences. The sequel gives an equally strong impression of the power of that inner world: Vance Weston having progressed to Europe, sits late at night on a balcony in the South of France:

He felt himself possessed by a brooding spirit of understanding, some mystic reassurance with sea and sky and life of men transmitted from sources deeper than reason. He had never been able to formulate it, but he had caught, in the pages of all the great creative writers, hints of that mysterious subjection and communion, impossible to define, but clear to the initiated as the sign exchanged between members of some secret brotherhood. (*GA* 187)

Edith Wharton shows her hero growing to trust the unfailing power of his inner world:

These alterations of mood, which he had once ascribed to instability of aim, no longer troubled him. He knew now that they were only the play of the world of images on his creative faculty, and that his fundamental self remained unchanged under such shifting impulses. By the time the train reached Nice he was so lost in the visionary architecture of his inner world that the other had become invisible. (*GA* 205)

The supernatural and divine nature of his inspiration continues to be affirmed: 'Vance was the instrument to which the goddess laid her lips' (*GA* 291), 'there was a dumb subterranean power in her that corresponded with his own sense of the forces by which his inventive faculty was fed' (*GA* 385); 'it was as though he were watching some obscure creative process, the whirl and buzz of the cosmic wheels' (*GA* 414).

Edith Wharton's use of mystical terminology is an attempt to convey an experience which takes place deep within the individual and which comes from an unknown source: the nature of that experience defies direct description and can only, from her standpoint in time, be conveyed through the language of the spirit, and through suggestion and symbol. Not only the language and symbols suggest that her concept of inspiration and imagination was Romantic: she gives 'Kubla Khan' an important role in Vance's early development. (His first article as a professional writer is 'Coleridge Today'.) On his first visit to 'The Willows' he finds a book open at the poem:

> Oh, what beautiful, what incredible words! What did they mean? But what did it matter what they meant? Or whether they meant anything but their own unutterable music? . . . It was a new music, a music utterly unknown to him, but to which the hidden chords of his soul at once vibrated. It was something for *him* – something that intimately belonged to him. (*HRB* 50)

Whatever else the poem may be about it is certainly concerned with the central experience of creation. Edith Wharton uses it as a catalyst in itself for Vance and as a symbol of his recognition of the creative force within himself. In so far as Coleridge's concept of the creative imagination, while associated with the creative power of God, is concerned with perception of nature and with the idea that the artist's creative power is a faculty common to humanity but intensified to such a degree in the artist that it becomes a divine gift, Edith Wharton appears to be in agreement. But she is not concerned with the revelation of a God as the power working through and behind nature and artistic creativity, nor with the discovery of the universal and permanent in itself, but only in so far as this enlarges the understanding and creativity of the individual artist; it is always the individual as he functions in the concretely realized outside world that is her central concern. The conscious minds of her artist heroes recognize in nature and great literature and art what their unconscious already knows, and the transcendental is a revelation of a power within themselves rather than of God.

The 'sources deeper than reason' within Vance that recognize and respond to Coleridge's poem and other works of literature, also respond to nature. The innate quality of the artist is part of great universal forces beyond the individual. Edith Wharton makes frequent references to the soul's 'mystic fusion' with something universal outside: the depths wtihin respond to 'some deep complementary power' in the universe. For Vance, the sea in particular awakens this response and stands as a symbol of what he has been deprived of in his childhood and boyhood in the Midwest, continuity with the past and with the universal timeless forces. When he reaches it at last after Frenside, his critic and mentor, has ridiculed his attempt to write about the sea without having seen it, he responds by feeling 'for the first time the weight of the universe upon him' and he plunges 'his hands into it, as if in dedication' (*HRB* 134). When he returns to the sea three years later on his honeymoon, his responses have become more conscious, the symbol more unmistakable:

As he stood there, all the shapes of beauty which had haunted his imagination seemed to rise from the sea and draw about him. They swept him upward into the faint dapplings of the morning sky, and he caught, as in a mystic vision, the meaning of beauty, the secret of poetry, the sense of the forces struggling in him for expression. (*HRB* 184)

Vance's sense that he is part of the continuous flow of the universe grows as does his ability to conceptualize his feelings. After his rejection by Halo:

the craving to see the sea swept over him again, vehement, uncontrollable, surging from the depths which held the source of things. He stood staring at his vision until it mastered him. . . . The wind was cold but Vance did not feel it. The old affinity woke in him, the sense of some deep complementary power moving those endless surges as it swayed his listening self. He dropped down on the beach and lay there, letting the night and the sea sweep through him on the wings of the passionate gale. He felt like a speck in those vast elemental hands, yet sure of himself and his future as a seed being swept to the cleft where it belonged. (*HRB* 324)

In *The Gods Arrive* his feelings of containing within himself a 'mysterious Sea of Being' which responds to the sense of timelessness symbolized by the actual sea grows with the development of his self-awareness. His departure from America for Europe is a symbolic as much as a real voyage back into the cultural and traditional past. In his thoughts he gropes towards a more complete understanding of the symbol, and measures his growth against it; he has travelled some distance from the point where he first contemplated the sea, but realizes that he cannot claim to have reached knowledge of the depths in his own nature which respond to the 'limitless freedom' and timelessness of the sea:

Vance sat with his arm about Halo brooding over the mystery of the waters and his own curious inability to feel their vastness as he had once felt it from a lonely beach on Long Island. It was as if the sea shrank when no land was visible – as if the absence of the familiar shore made it too remote, too abstract, to reach his imagination. He had a feeling that perhaps he would never be able to assimilate perfection or completeness. (*GA* 17)

As he becomes surer in understanding and control of his creative faculty, he also trusts his feeling of identity with the universal in nature and with writers of the past.

Eventually when he runs away from his two women, Floss 'the one that his soul rejected and his body yearned for' and Halo 'who had once seemed the answer to all he asked of life, but had now faded to a reproach and a torment', into the wilds, Vance understands 'the magic power of continuity' which he had first sensed that he needed by the sea. The sea and nature provide him with a sense of 'the rhythmic beat of the universe'; 'The Willows' and Europe provide him with an understanding of the cultural past. The artist's imagination needs to feed on natural continuity and on the artefacts of human history. Only when Vance can see himself clearly as an individual and can return to the world, and also as merely part of the continuous process in nature and art, can 'the Gods arrive' and can he realize himself as a writer. The two sides of his life, the inner and the outer, must be reconciled.

> Vance understood that he would never be able to rest long in evasion or refusal, that something precise and productive must come out of each step in his life. He began to think of himself less as a small unsatisfied individual than as an instrument in some mighty hand; and one day he was seized by the desire to put this rush of returning energy into words . . . his new book was shaping itself in a mood of deep spiritual ardour such as his restless intelligence had never before attained, and these weeks outside of time gave him his first understanding of the magic power of continuity. (GA 415–6)

A dose of St Augustine and fever complete his development towards maturity in his acceptance of pain:

> His physical suffering and helplessness seemed to have matured his mind. . . . Saint Augustine's words came back to him: 'Become a man and thou shalt feed on Me'; and he felt that at last he was ready to taste of the food of the full-grown however bitter to the lips it might be. (GA 421)

He has a moment of self-doubt when he meets Halo again: 'I'm not fit for you yet, Halo; I'm only just learning how to walk', but she gives him the link necessary for his integration with 'continuity' by telling him of his firm link with the future, their child. Vance recognizes that he is indissolubly part of the inexorable progress of time. The creative artist must accept the universal depths within himself, and the agitations of his inner life and his life in the world, if he is to achieve fulfilment: 'The gods approve / The depth and not the tumult of the soul.'

* * *

Dick Thaxter, hero of *Literature*, is clearly revealed as Vance's predecessor when he takes a walk in Central Park after the first reading of his play and feels himself in accord with nature and part of the universe:

> Darkness had dropped on it from a remote sky hung with the first stars. The air was still, but so buoyant that it seemed to bubble at his lips, and as he walked on between black shrubberies and the bare tracery of trees he had again his own boyish sense of being absorbed into the immense and palpitating night. It was a feeling he had never been able to define or to trace to its beginning: he knew only that sometimes, when his individual life was at its tensest, a tremendous hand seemed suddenly to seize and plunge him into the general sea of being. He abandoned himself now to its mysterious waves, thought and perception dancing on them like straws on the tide, while he pressed on farther into the night. (*LIT* Dr2 p. 66)

And once again there is a correspondence with the young Edith Wharton as she saw her self looking back:

> Yet what I recall of those rambles is not so much the comradeship of the other children, or the wise and friendly talk of our guide, as my secret sensitiveness to the landscape – something in me quite incommunicable to others, that was tremblingly and inarticulately awake to every detail of wind-warped fern and wide-eyed briar rose, yet more profoundly alive to a unifying magic beneath the diversities of the visible scene – a power with which I was in deep and solitary communion whenever I was alone with nature . . . and it has never since been still. (*BG* 54)

The most important symbol used by Edith Wharton in *Hudson River Bracketed* and *The Gods Arrive* to convey the 'sources deeper than reason' in her artist is borrowed from Goethe: that of 'The Mothers'. Whereas in her use of the sea, nature, 'The Willows', and Europe, the physical stands for a concept or concepts, 'The Mothers' is a multi-faceted concept which represents all the ideas which she sought to convey by symbols – Europe is an ideal because it contains the visible signs of culture and tradition in its art. Further, the concept of 'The Mothers' represents the depths within the individual artist which he must have the courage to plumb if he is to recognize his inmost resources, related to primordial and eternal forces in the universe, and if he is to bring to his art wisdom and understanding from those deepest sources. In Goethe's *Faust II*, Faust descends to The Mothers and invokes them:

> In your name Mothers, ye who on your throne
> In Endless space forever dwell alone
> Yet not alone! Around your heads float whirring
> The images of life – though lifeless, ever stirring
> What once has been in all its radiancy;
> Is there astir, eternal it would be. (Faust: Part Two, Act I)

Vance first comes across *Faust* in the library at 'The Willows' when he is planning his second novel *Instead* and after he has had some experience of the literary world of New York:

> Vance was more and more conscious of some deep-seated difference that cut him off from the circumambient literary 'brightness', or rather left him unsatisfied by it. . . . These brilliant verbal gymnastics – or the staccato enumeration of a series of physical aspects and sensations – they all left him with the sense of an immense emptiness underneath, just where in his own vision of the world, the deep forces stirred and wove men's fate. If he couldn't express that in his books he'd rather chuck it. . . . Some of the novels people talked about most excitedly – *Price of Meat*, say, already in its seventieth thousand, or *Egg Omelette*, which had owed its start to pulpit denunciations[6] and the quarrel of a Prize Committee over its exact degree of indecency – well, he had begun both books with enthusiasm, as their authors appeared to have; and then, at a certain point, had felt the hollowness underfoot, and said to himself: 'No, life's not like that, people are not like that. *The real stuff is way down, not on surface.' When he got hold of Faust at the Willows, and came to the part about the mysterious Mothers, moving in the subterranean depths among the primal forms of life, he shouted out: 'That's it – the fellows that write those books are all Motherless!'* (*HRB* 245; my italics)

Vance is here a standard-bearer for Edith Wharton's elderly disapproval of the modern American novel and the lack of discrimination of the public and critics, but she also shows Vance struggling toward an explanation of his uneasiness with his contemporaries and seizing on the symbol of the Mothers as a representation of his unfocused and confused thoughts. It is easy to be diverted by the heavy irony in the passage quoted here, but Edith Wharton is attempting to portray the origins of true creativity, to express the inexpressible, by a combination of symbol and the presentation of an individual artist's particular experience. Simultaneously she writes from the prejudiced standpoint of an ageing writer out of touch with the new generation of writers and from that of a creative artist conscious of creative power. Possibly the strident note which can be heard in Vance's thoughts on the subject of New York literary salons betrays a frustration not only with the current fashion in fiction but with her own inability to write much better, although the fact that she included *The Children*, *Hudson River Bracketed* and *The Gods Arrive* among her own favourite novels seems to point to a blindness about the quality of her later work.

That 'The Mothers' symbolize the infinite and universal available to all humanity, not only the artist, and that her use of religious terminology to describe inspiration is not fortuitous, is made clear in the following passage:

He thought himself back onto the porch at Crampton, smelt the
neglected lilies, heard the jangle of the Euphoria trolley, and his grandmother saying: 'Don't a day like this make you feel as if you could get to
God right through that blue up there?' He remembered having answered,
rather petulantly, he didn't feel as if anything would take him near God;
but now he was at least nearer to understanding what she had meant.
Perhaps what she called 'God' was the same as what he called 'The
Mothers' – that mysterious Sea of Being of which the dark reaches
swayed and rumoured in his soul . . . perhaps one symbol was as good as
another to figure the imperceptible point where the fleeting human
consciousness touches Infinity . . . (*HRB* 327)

The Mothers, as the archetypal images of the eternal and limitless, are
related to personal inspiration of the artist through the necessity for
him to reach deep into the roots of his own being which lie both in his
own past and in the universe as a whole. Vance eventually realizes
that he cannot discard his roots which he has grown to see as
impoverished and ill-nourished but that he must accept them as part
of himself, and that, however antipathetic to all he has learned to
value, they too are part of that universal whole. The moment comes
when he has returned as a celebrity to read his latest novel *Colossus* in
his home town Euphoria:

How attentive they were, how hushed! As usual, the wings of his
imagination lifted him above moral contingencies, and his voice soared
over the outspread silence. But gradually he began to be conscious of the
dense nonconductive quality of that silence, of the fact that not a word he
said traversed its impenetrable medium. The men were fidgeting in their
seats like children in church; the women were openly consulting their
pocket-mirrors. A programme dropped from the gallery, and every head
was turned to see it fall. Vance could hear his voice flagging and groping
as he hurried on from fragment, to fragment. . . . Which was it now? Ah:
the descent of the Mothers, the crux, the centre of the book. He had put
the whole of himself into that scene – and his self had come out of
Euphoria, been conceived and fashioned there, made of the summer heat
on endless wheat fields, the frozen winter skies, the bell of the Roman
Catholic Church ringing through the stillness, on nights when he
couldn't sleep, after the last trolley-rattle had died out; the plants budding
along the ditches on the way to Crampton, the fiery shade of the elm-
grove down by the river . . . he had been made out of all this, and there, in
the rows before him, sat his native protoplasm, and wriggled in its seats,
and twitched at his collar-buttons, and didn't understand him. . . . And at
last it was over, and the theatre rang and rang with the grateful applause
of the released . . . (*GA* 386–7)

Vance's emotional descent to The Mothers, out of which experience
he wrote the scene in *Colossus*, occurs near the beginning of *The Gods
Arrive* when he and Halo are in a cathedral in Spain:

'The place is as big as that sky out there', he murmured. He and Halo moved forward. First one colonnade, low-vaulted and endless, drew them on; then another. They were caught in a dim network of architectural forms, perpetually repeated abstractions of the relations between arch and shaft. The similarity of what surrounded them was so confusing that they could not be sure if they had passed from one colonnade to another, or if the whole system were revolving with them around some planetary centre still invisible. *Vance felt as if he had dropped over the brim of things into the mysterious world where straight lines loop themselves into curves. He thought: 'It's like the feel of poetry, just as it's beginning to be born in you' – that fugitive moment before words restrict the vision.* But he gave up the struggle for definitions.

The obscure central bulk about which those perpetual aisles revolved gradually took shape as sculptured walls rising high overhead. In the walls were arched openings; lights reflected in polished marble glimmered through the foliation of wrought-iron gates. Vance was as excited and exhausted as if he had raced for miles over the uneven flagging. Suddenly he felt the desire to lift his arms and push back the overwhelming spectacle till he had the strength to receive it. He caught Halo's arm. 'Come away' he said hoarsely. . . . They began to walk down one of the aisles. Farther and farther away in the heart of the shadows they left the great choir and altar; yet they seemed to get no nearer to the door. Halo stood still again. 'No – this way', she said, with the abruptness of doubt. 'We're going in the wrong direction.' *Vance remembered a passage in the Second Faust which had always haunted him: the scene where Faust descends to the Mothers.* 'He must have wound round and round like this', he thought. They had turned and were walking down another low-vaulted vista toward a glow-worm light at its end. This led to a door bolted and barred on the inner side, and evidently long unopened. 'It's not that.' They turned again and walked in the deepening darkness down another colonnade. *Vance thought of the Cretan labyrinth, of Odysseus evoking the mighty dead, of all the subterranean mysteries on whose outer crust man loves and fights and dies.* The blood was beating in his ears. He began to wish that they might never find the right door, but *go on turning about forever at the dark heart of things.* (*GA* 21–3; my italics)

Vance, like Faust, has to go down the primordial roots of humanity and self, before he can conjure up what he most desires; an ideal beauty and form. The range of reference of which Vance's mind is now capable demonstrates how far he has travelled from the state of ignorance which he betrays to Halo near the beginning of *Hudson River Bracketed* when he takes her allusion to Delphi to mean the Delphi of The First Church of Christ, USA. To reach the degree of self-knowledge which is represented by his symbolic descent to The Mothers, and from which he can assimilate later in *The Gods Arrive* his personal past, Vance, short for Advance, has paradoxically had to retreat further and further back into the past. This journey begins with 'The Willows': ironically, this is not an old house to anyone other than a barbarian from the West,[7] and the style in which it is built, the symbolic title of the novel, epitomizes a type of American provincialism despised by Edith Wharton. Vance learns in the first novel that an artist cannot afford to remain ignorant of cultural tradition, and in the second that he cannot dismiss his own past: continuity with the universal and personal past is vital. *Hudson River Bracketed* shows Vance's journey away from his own roots towards a wider culture; *The Gods Arrive* shows also his journey down towards an understanding of what he has learned, and of the source of inspiration. In *The Gods Arrive* we have more internal monologue and self-examination than in its predecessor. Vance learns to discriminate between his genuinely inspired work and the superficial; after the critics have acclaimed his second successful novel he thinks:

> The thing had come too easily; he knew it had not been fetched up out of the depths . . . when he was alone he recalled the passionate groping conviction with which he had written 'Instead' and the beginning of the unfinished novel, 'Magic', and the feeling returned that those two books had been made out of his inmost substance, while the new one sprang from its surface. 'The Puritan in Spain' was better written and more adroitly composed than its predecessors; there were scenes . . . that Vance could not re-read without a certain pleasure. These scenes had assuredly been written with the same conviction as those in the earlier books; yet now he felt only their superior craft. . . . 'What's the use of doing anything really big? If I ever do, nobody'll read it. . . . Well, and what if they don't? Who am I writing for anyhow? Only the Mothers!' (*GA* 74)

He grows to trust that the fount of his inspiration will never dry up: 'at the moment when he felt his creative faculty slipping away from him forever, there it stood at his side, as though in mockery of his self-distrust' (*GA* 121). And in an ecstasy of creation he realizes that his hard apprenticeship has been necessary:

> He recalled the old days of his poverty and obscurity in New York, when he had sat alone in his fireless boarding-house room, pouring out prose and poetry till his brain reeled with hunger and fatigue; and he knew now that those hours had been the needful prelude to whatever he had accomplished since. 'You have to go plumb down to the Mothers to fish up the real thing', he though exultantly. (*GA* 121)

* * *

If Edith Wharton's concept of 'inspiration' seems romantic and imprecise, it is undeniable that there is a process which takes place in the unconscious which is largely inexplicable and inexpressible. Arthur Koestler in *The Act of Creation* devotes a chapter to showing

> that the unconscious is neither a romantic nor a mystic fancy, but a working concept in the absence of which nearly every event of mental life would have to be regarded as a miracle. There is nothing very romantic about the wheels of the railway carriage screaming 'I told you so'; it is simply an observed fact. (p. 318)

The concept of the unconscious existed before the twentieth century: L.L. Whyte concludes his book *The Unconscious Before Freud*: 'It cannot be disputed that by 1870–1880 the general conception of the unconscious mind was a European commonplace.' The idea would be familiar to Edith Wharton from Goethe if from no other source:

> Man cannot persist long in a conscious state, he must throw himself back into the unconscious, for his root lives there. . . . Take for example a talented musician composing an important score: consciousness and unconsciousness will be like warp and weft. (Goethe, Letter to Humboldt, 17 March 1832)

A modern affirmation of the existence of a mysterious creative process that takes place in the unconscious comes from Graham Greene's author hero, Bendrix, in *The End of the Affair*:

> So much in writing depends on the superficiality of one's days. One may be preoccupied with shopping and income tax returns and chance conversations, but the stream of the unconscious continues to flow undisturbed, solving problems, planning ahead: one sits down sterile and dispirited at the desk, and suddenly the words come as though from air: the situations that seemed blocked in a hopeless impasse move forward: the work has been done while one slept or shopped or talked with friends. (p. 20)

> So much of a novelist's writing, as I have said takes place in the unconscious: in those depths the last word is written before the first word appears on paper. We remember details of our story, we do not invent them. (p. 35)

Edith Wharton would find little to disagree with in this description: her own attempt to describe what takes place in 'some secret region on the sheer edge of consciousness' in her fiction about the writer succeeds in conveying not only the essentially mysterious quality of one phase of the creative act but also the feeling of exhilaration and power that it brings the artist.

Clearly, Edith Wharton's plot and 'illuminating incidents' in the Vance Weston novels are contrived to illustrate her precepts: one of the most imperative of these, as has been seen in Chapter One, was that taste is 'the regulating principle' of the art of living as well as of all art, and 'it is the atmosphere in which art lives, and outside of which it cannot live' (*FW* 40–1). She felt that the artist in particular must be educated to exercise taste and discrimination (as will be shown more fully· in Chapter Five). Because the function of the creative imagination is to re-create and transform experience, the quality of the artist's perception must be cultivated. She stresses the importance of her artist–hero's aesthetic education and development throughout the two novels. He is shown from the beginning to have a genuine creative impulse and the innate ability to transmute personal experience into literature, but to need breadth of experience both to develop taste and to provide him with material to transmute into art. Vance is conscious of the poverty of his experience early in his career:

> After the first few lines, which almost wrote themselves, the inspiration died out, or rather he felt that he didn't know what to say next – that if his mind had contained more of the stuff of experience words would have flocked of their own accord for its expression. He supposed it must take a good deal of experience to furnish the material for even a few lines of poetry. (*HRB* 41)

Edith Wharton emphasizes that one of Vance's strengths is his eagerness to seek new intellectual, artistic and social experience to feed his creative imagination, and the story of his developing taste illustrates her belief in the importance of education. The inner impulse is not enough; the artist needs nourishment as well as stimulus from outside experience. The artist needs to submerge himself in life: Frenside tells Vance:

> The artist has got to feed his offspring out of his own tissue. Enrich that, day and night – perpetually. . . . I suppose you go out a good deal these days – see a good many people? A novelist ought to. . . . Manners are your true material, after all. (*HRB* 287)

At the same time, he needs to educate his perception of the world through experience of books and art. This dual aim is a central concern of the two novels, *Hudson River Bracketed* and *The Gods Arrive*, and of *Literature*.

Edith Wharton dramatizes her belief in the necessity for the writer to develop his mind and to open himself to experience and, moreover, to traditional values by taking as her hero a young man from what she sees as a particularly intellectually and socially impoverished background, that of the American Midwest, and showing the gradual development of his mind and imagination as he experiences the world. Vance's story (as will be shown) illustrates and illuminates Edith Wharton's long-held views on the importance of education, tradition and order, and on the poverty of American culture as well as her ideas on the nature and needs of the creative writer based firmly on her own experiences.

Vance's journey, actual and symbolic, from Euphoria, Illinois to the salons of Paris and London is powered by his hunger for knowledge and experience. He wants from his youth in the Midwest to 'be a writer, and if possible a poet' but one of the first lessons he learns when he goes east is that his innate inclination is not enough and that his ignorance, previously unsuspected by him, is a hindrance. Even while he is still at home he feels alienated from the values of his family and after his illness feels an 'awful sense of loneliness'. This sense of apartness is seen by Edith Wharton as an inherent character-istic of the artist. She tells of her own preference as a child for being alone, and as an adult she retreated each morning to her 'secret garden' to emerge only in the afternoons to enjoy the company of her friends and the diversions of society. She felt 'different' from the companions of her youth. Vance, even in the earliest days of his marriage, is detached enough to think: 'From his childhood there had been in him an irreducible core of selfishness . . . a hidden cave in which he hoarded his secretest treasures' (*HRB* 200). Dick Thaxter too feels detached from his surroundings. By going east Vance demonstrates his instinct for a culture that will enable him to express his visions and, quite as importantly, it will widen and alter the scope of his imagination.

Vance's awareness of his deficiencies begins when he visits 'The Willows'. Previously, when he first arrives in Paul's Landing, he sees it with the eyes of Euphoria and is shocked by the lack of amenities:

> Paul's Landing was like a place that enterprise of every sort had passed by, as if all its inhabitants had slept through the whole period of industrial development which Vance Weston had been taught to regard as humanity's supreme achievement. If Euphoria values were the right ones – and he had no others to replace them with – then the people who did not strive for them were predestined down-and-outers, as repugnant to the religion of business as the thief and the adulterer to the religion of Christianity. (*HRB* 37)

He quickly learns, through his imaginative power of perceiving the value of the past, that Euphoria values are sterile and shallow. His reassessment of his education and background is triggered off by the 'old' house. One of the ways in which the past influences the present is through buildings, as Edith Wharton's travel books point out.

Vance's values begin to adjust as he stands beneath the portrait of Miss Lorburn in the room that has remained unchanged since she lived there:

> The past – they all belonged to the past, this woman and her house, to the same past, a past of their own, a past so remote from anything in Vance Weston's experience that it took its place in history anywhere in the dark Unknown before Euphoria was. (*HRB* 49)

His visits to the library of 'The Willows' rapidly bring home to him the depth of his deprivation: 'The pressure of this weight of wisdom on his ignorance was suffocating.' He thinks that 'what he needed, no doubt, to enter that world, was *education* – the very thing he thought he already had!' He is momentarily overwhelmed by the task of achieving education:

> He had been brought up in the creed that there was nothing a fellow from Euphoria, the cradle of all the Advantages, couldn't attain to. Only – how? It seemed to him that the gulf was untraversable. If only he could have been left alone in that library, left there for half a year, perhaps . . . But even so, he felt that he needed some kind of tuition to prepare him for the library. The Past was too big, too complicated, too aloof, to surrender its secrets so lightly. (*HRB* 95)

His instinct 'which always made him seize on what was meant for his own nourishment' makes him realize that his only hope for gaining the education he needs lies 'in returning as often as he could to this silent room, and trying to hack a way through the dense jungle of the past'. This source of knowledge is soon denied him by his banishment from Paul's Landing and he resorts to the New York public library, where he plunges into an orgy of reading:

> his hours at the library were so engrossing, and his ignorance had revealed itself on a scale so unsuspected and overwhelming that each day drew him back to the lion-guarded gates of knowledge. . . . Drifting from dream to dream, eating daily less, studying daily for longer hours, he entered into the state of strange illumination which comes to ardent youth when the body hungers while the intelligence is fed. (*HRB* 126)

Edith Wharton's own education was almost as haphazard as Vance's but she was fortunate in having access to her father's 'gentleman's library'. Her German governess fed her 'with all the wealth of German literature' – this influence is apparent in her writing – and she adds 'but for this, and the leave to range in my father's library, my mind would have starved at the age when the mental muscles are most in need of feeding' (*BG* 48). Although as she says 'by the time I was seventeen, though I had not read every book in my father's library, I had looked into them all' (*BG* 71), she had been deprived of a methodical education and was only to fill in some of the gaps through the help of Egerton Winthrop after she was married: 'It was too late for me to acquire the mental discipline I had missed in the schoolroom, but my new friend directed and systemized my reading, and filled some of the worst gaps in my education' (*BG* 94).

Dick Thaxter too as a youth at Harvard seeks nourishment from books:

> It was the period of his most ravenous reading: he plunged into books as into a magic lengthening of experience. There were hours when it seemed to him that literature contained all art and all beauty: when each word was a dewdrop reflecting a whole landscape and the reading of a single phrase was like entering the colonnade of a mighty temple. (*LIT* Dr2 p. 67)

In *The Gods Arrive* Vance is seen as a writer not as a reader; the stage of insatiable intellectual curiosity has passed. A period of intensive reading is vital for the development of the mind of the writer; books also act as direct stimulus to the creative artist. For the child Edith 'this ferment of reading revived my story-telling fever; but now I wanted to write and not to improvise' (*BG* 73); for the child Dicky 'the day came when he wanted to make his own books instead of reading them' (*LIT* Dr2 p. 20); for the young Vance coming from the library 'his shaking fingers filled page after page with verse and prose' (*HRB* 126).

However essential books are in the education of the artist, people and experience of life itself are equally important to the development of his creative imagination. People are always important to Edith Wharton: 'Books are alive enough to an imagination which knows how to animate them; but living companions are more living still' (*BG* 92). Vance realizes that 'a raw boy whose experience was bounded by a rooming house and a library' would not be able to write a great novel. He, for all his ignorance, is contrasted favourably with the educated people he comes across, from the Spears and their circle in America to Alders in Spain, from the group in Paris to the group in London. Even Frenside is deficient in that he lacks the creative gift: 'the critical faculty outweighed all others in him'. Lewis Tarrant, Halo's husband, is set up in apposition to Vance. He typifies the cultivated and cold men who people Edith Wharton's novels – it is impossible not to see Walter Berry as the original of this type – for while he possesses the intellect desired by Vance he lacks emotional fire and creative energy. Halo thinks about him: 'he had a real love of books, a calm cultivated interest in art; his mind was like a chilly moonlit reflection of her own' (*HRB* 362). Halo contrasts him with Vance in the house she shares with Tarrant as his wife:

> He stretched his hands to the flame, and as she watched him she remembered, a few days before, looking at Lewis's hands as he held them out in the same way, and thinking: 'Why isn't he a poet?'. . . . This boy's hands were different: sturdier – less diaphanous, with blunter fingertips, though the fingers were long and flexible. A worker's hand, she thought: a maker's hand. (*HRB* 167)

Vance, of course, possesses the vital ingredient for a 'maker', the impulse and talent to create. But he needs in addition to nourishment for his starved mind the direct stimulus of new people and places. The second-hand experiences of literature need to be extended by first-hand experiences of life to widen his knowledge of the world and to act as a trigger for his imagination. Vance has, as much as his intellectual curiosity, an 'irresistible force which drove him in pursuit of the food his imagination required'.

The longing for stimulating and congenial people was felt by Edith Wharton in her young-womanhood:

> I was overmastered by the longing to meet people who shared my interests. . . . What I wanted above all was to get to know other writers, to be welcomed among people who lived for the things I had always secretly lived for. I knew only one novelist, Paul Bourget . . . [he] was always . . . telling me that at the formative stage of my career I ought to be with people who were thinking and creating. Egerton Winthrop was too generous not to come round also to this view, and in the end it was he who urged my husband to go to London with me for a few weeks every year, so that I might at least meet a few men of letters, and have a taste of an old society in which the various elements had been fused for generations. (*BG* 123)

Part of Halo's attraction for Vance lies in her apparently holding the key to the knowledge of the past that Vance desires; another part lies in the fact that she is different from any of the other women he has known:

> In the world of Euphoria and the Tracys the women did nothing but ask questions. They never stopped asking questions. . . . With Mrs Tarrant it was different. She had a way of dashing straight at essentials. And anyhow, she didn't seem to care how Vance spent his time when he was away from her. (*HRB* 260)

But, as with Laura Lou who quickly sank from being the inspirer of Vance's work to being 'the insuperable obstacle to its fulfillment', Halo in turn becomes an impediment rather than a stimulus:

> He had imagined that once he was at work Halo's presence would be the only stimulus he needed; and no doubt it was, since the book had been written. But he had not felt her indignation flaming through him as it had when they used to meet at The Willows. The dampening effect of habit seemed to have extinguished that flame. (*GA* 74)

Vance consciously brackets Halo with Laura Lou in his mind in Paris:

> Communion with Halo had once been the completion of his dreams; now, when his thoughts took flight, she was the obstacle that arrested them. When he thought of her he felt almost as hopeless of explaining himself as he had with Laura Lou. (*GA* 78)

He turns to new friends for intellectual companionship and criticism of his work – and to Floss Delaney for sex – 'it was not his fault or hers if the deep workings of his imagination were no longer roused by her [Halo's] presence' (*GA* 111). Halo eventually says to him after he has returned to her the first time: 'Perhaps the real change you need . . . is not a new place but a new woman.'

Vance is as much a ruthless opportunist in his way as Undine Spragge in *The Custom of the Country* is in hers, for he not only quickly realizes how he must adapt to further his own ends but uses the people he meets for his own enrichment. Like Undine he never relates to anyone in his life on a profound level. The three women in his lfe, Laura Lou, Halo and Floss, appear to serve as symbols for Vance as much as they do for the reader. Laura Lou stands for emotion and romantic love, and fails to satisfy Vance's other needs; Halo stands for reason and intellect and appears to Vance as a 'goddess' and 'custodian of the unknown'; and Floss stands for physical desire. Halo – and the intellect – holds a far larger section of the stage than do the other two, for she plays a continuous role in the plot, her consciousness serves as a window for a view of Vance, and Vance in his maturity returns to her. As with the apposition of May Welland and Ellen Olenska in *The Age of Innocence*, representing respectively American innocence and European experience, the characters seem to be fulfilling roles rather than fulfilling the criterion laid down by Edith Wharton that they should 'live'. Neither a symmetrical nor a symbolic placing automatically disqualifies a character from coming to life, but to do so that character must be seen to possess and to demonstrate some individuality. As Edith Wharton says:

The novelist's permanent problem is that of making his people at once typical and individual, universal and particular, and in adopting the form of the novel of situation he perpetually runs the risk of upsetting that nice balance of attributes unless he persists in thinking of his human beings first, and of their predicament only as the outcome of what they are. (*WF* 143)

Even Halo, the most fully realized of Vance's women, only exists to provide him with support and inspiration. The tension between her role and her individuality is never satisfactorily explored. She exists to provide Vance with a route to education, and to underline his needs and his genius. But her attempts, after the initial development has taken place and his intellectual hunger abated, to educate him in a formal way are rejected. She takes him to Chartres – as she had led him to 'the most erudite works on Spain' – and he 'felt nothing, saw nothing'. When he first arrives in Europe in his quest for a deeper and richer past than America could offer him, he is overwhelmed by new experiences: 'When the impressions were too abundant and powerful they benumbed him' (*GA* 38). Halo finds that:

the bright confusion of his mind sometimes charmed and sometimes frightened her. . . . Sometimes she asked herself if it would not have been better if they had stayed in America, in some out-of-the-way place where this tremendous vision of a new world would not have thrust itself between him and his work. Yet she felt that it must be a weak talent that could not bear the shock of wonder and the hardening processes of experience. Presently the mass of new impressions would be sorted out and dominated by his indefatigable mind, and become part of his material. (*GA* 41)

As Edith Wharton planned for Dick Thaxter a 'wonder-year' in Europe during which he writes nothing and so offends his patron, Silmore, but which is an important 'fallow time' for the developing artist, so for Vance the early period in Europe is unproductive but vital to his development: 'this journey was a time of preparation from which his imagination would come forth richer and more vigorous' (*GA* 48). Vance is successively fascinated by and then rejects the values of the groups he meets: his sturdy instinct enables him to distinguish the true from the meretricious and he takes from people only what he needs to nourish his imagination. Even when he despises the company he accepts it as useful material: 'And instantly he began to weave the whole scene into "Loot", his heart beating excitedly as he felt himself swept along on the strong current of the human comedy' (*HRB* 309). Each book of *The Gods Arrive* marks a stage in Vance's exploration of the outer world which increases the richness of his inner world: Book One is set in Spain, Book Two in Paris, Book Three in the South of France, Book Four in London, and the final book back in America. While at first, 'his impulse was either to try to incorporate every fresh suggestion, visual or imaginative into the fabric of his work', he learns to order his impressions and to use them.

Vance's periods of stimulation by people and places alternate with periods of withdrawal: 'To look and listen and question was as stimulating as creation. Then as always, he began to feel the need of setting his mind to work on the new material he had amassed, away from the excitement of discussion' (*GA* 78). In this mood he thinks 'what were cities and societies for but to sterilize the imagination?' (*GA* 116). But Edith Wharton shows that her artist cannot remain apart from the world, his material, for long.

As Vance travels through Europe, Edith Wharton shows the predatory nature of the artist feeding not only off the social groups he encounters but, more reprehensibly, off individuals. These characters are created in order to highlight aspects of the artist. For example, Vance finds among the 'drifting fragments' of the expatriate British community in the South of France a vulnerable young man who is a pale reflection of Vance's younger self. Chris Churley serves as a device for pointing out the difference between the true artist and the dilettante and within the world of the novel as someone for the hero to argue with and 'develop the muscles of his ideas'. Vance is aware that he is using the young man to stimulate his imagination without giving much in return:

> His inspiration, which had begun to flag before Chris Churley's appear-
> ance, now flowed with a strong regular beat. The poor boy's talk had
> done for Vance what Vance's society had failed to do for him. Vance
> knew that his creative faculty had grown strong enough to draw stimulus
> from contradiction instead of being disturbed by it. (*GA* 187)

Vance takes what he needs from Churley and, although he recognizes his duty to help him, fails him because a newer and more interesting person – Floss Delaney – appears. Churley's death underlines the predatoriness of the artistic character which must sacrifice altruism to growth in experience. Vance suffers, unattractively, not from failing Churley but from failing to conquer Floss Delaney; not from betraying his near-self, but from being betrayed by his deeper self:

> It was useless to tell himself that now he knew the world he could place
> her without difficulty, could class her as the trivial beauty whom any
> intelligent man would weary of in a week. . . . Vance knew that there
> were selves under selves in him, and that one of the undermost belonged
> to Floss Delaney. (*GA* 264)

Floss's function in the novel – paradoxically for she herself is impervious to deep emotion – is to teach the hero the meaning of suffering. At the beginning of his career she is the catalyst for his first story, 'One Day', and at the end she brings about his final metamorphosis into the complete artist who accepts himself and the world outside.

Vance's journey to London, which means at first 'change and freedom', highlights the potential for escapism in 'change' and for delusion in professional and emotional notions of 'freedom'. Halo points this out for the reader: she wonders 'whether a change of scene – figurative as well as actual – might not be increasingly necessary to him' (GA 340). England marks the last stage in Vance's odyssey and he returns to America. His experiences in the Old World have changed the raw boy from Euphoria and his mind and imagination have been enriched and expanded. His emotional ties with the New World are finally severed after his grandmother's death and his disillusionment with Floss, and he withdraws from society and 'broods' upon his grandmother's dying words: 'Maybe we haven't made enough of pain – been too afraid of it. Don't be afraid of it' (GA 409). Through his study of St Augustine he comes to understand her advice and realizes that he must accept suffering in order 'to become a man'. When he emerges reborn into the world, he is ready to 'taste the food of the full-grown' and vows he will be 'ruled by realities not illusions' (GA 417). His education has been completed through suffering both as a man and as an artist. Halo recognizes that he is now grown-up and that his imagination is, finally, a fit vehicle for his innate genius.

As has been seen, Edith Wharton thought little of the novel that reproduced a 'slice-of-life': 'transmutation is the first principle of art, and copying can never be a substitute for creative vision' (TMF). The artist's experiences are transformed by his creative imagination through 'inward brooding'. She repeatedly comes back to this idea in *The Writing of Fiction*:

> As to experience, intellectual and moral, the creative imagination can make a little go a long way, provided it remains long enough in the mind and is sufficiently brooded upon. One good heartbreak will furnish the poet with many songs, and the novelist with a considerable number of novels. (WF 21)[8]

But of course 'the mind which would bring this secret germ to fruition must be able to nourish it with an accumulated wealth of knowledge and experience' (WF 18). She shows Vance gaining this knowledge and experience, and 'in the intervals he needed time to brood on his themes, to let them round themselves within him' (*HRB* 199). He comes home from his ventures into the world of art and people 'laden with treasure to be transmuted into the flesh and blood of his creations' (*HRB* 381). In *The Gods Arrive* Vance's consciousness is seen in 'that state of inward brooding when the visible world becomes a blank' (*GA* 80).[9] Edith Wharton shows her artist's imagination fired by the scenes around him and transforming those scenes into a unique vision: 'Visions and images pressed on him. They mingled with the actual scene, so that what he saw, and what his fancy made of it, flowed into one miracle of night and fire' (*GA* 219).

Edith Wharton's concept of the creative imagination incorporates the mystical and the secular, the innate power and acquired experience. She shows in her fiction as she does in her autobiography that the artist's mind and perceptions must be developed before he can use his inspiration, and that inspiration itself is partly powered by outside experience and partly by a force within him that comes from unknown depths.

Method in Practice: A Study of *Literature*, *Hudson River Bracketed* and *The Gods Arrive*

I have chosen as an example of how Edith Wharton constructed a novel her unfinished and unpublished work, *Literature*, which is among her papers at the Beinecke Library at Yale University. The reasons for choosing this novel from the abundance at Yale are, firstly, because successive stages from the earliest notes to the final version exist; secondly, because it contains examples of how she transmutes her own experiences into fiction; thirdly, because, as will become clear, it is an early version of *Hudson River Bracketed* and *The Gods Arrive* which dramatize her views on the inner nature and attributes of the writer and on the essential external influences on his creative life. *Literature*, which she worked on before the war, affords simultaneously an example of her method of constructing a novel, which may be compared with her theory of fiction, of the relationship between her experience and her art and of her opinions in fictional form about the creative process. Her reasons, stated and deduced, for abandoning *Literature* and reforming her *Künstlerroman* into the two Vance Weston novels published in 1929 and 1932, relate to her views on the problems for the artist in reconciling his inner and outer worlds which become more acute in the disorder of the postwar world. From the evidence of the genesis of *Literature* we have a portrait of Edith Wharton as an artist: from the three novels *Literature*, *Hudson River Bracketed* and *The Gods Arrive*, we have her portrait of an artist.

There are four stages of the unpublished novel:

(1) A manuscript notebook containing notes (Appendix I), a scenario at the back (Appendix II), and chapter summaries (Appendix III).
(2) 69 pages of manuscript, numbered 91–114, which correspond to

the last page of Chapter V, Book I, up to the end of Chapter VI; 80–93, which corresponds to the beginning of Chapter VII, Book II, to the middle of Chapter VII; 115–43, which corresponds to the middle of Chapter VII to the end of Chapter IX (Appendix IV).

(3) 44 pages of typescript with ms corrections of Chapters I–V (Except the last page) referred to as Draft I (Appendix V).

(4) A typescript of both the manuscript (which is Book II and the final Chapter of Book I) and Draft I (Book I except for Chapter VI) which incorporates the manuscript corrections. This typescript is referred to as Draft II (Appendix VI).

Within the notebook, the most interesting of the four stages, are three distinct steps in the planning of the novel from notes to a scenario to detailed chapter summaries. The notes are written in various inks and pencils, with one typed sheet gummed in which has a note in red ink at the side: 'keep for Man of Genius'. These notes appear to be random thoughts around the theme of life and development of a writer, jotted down at various moments over a period of time (which can be dated) and later worked into the detailed scenario. I have grouped extracts from them in the first Appendix in the following way: ideas for plot and character; short descriptions of scenery and characters and their feelings; phrases, sentences and aphorisms, sometimes attached to a character; paragraphs of narration; quotations from other authors; sentences of dialogue; sentences and paragraphs about literature or writing.

The date when she began work on *Literature*, although she had presumably 'brooded' upon the central situation beforehand, is not in doubt. On the outside of the notebook underneath the barely discernible title, 'A Man of Genius'[1], is the date 1913, and on the flyleaf: 'Dresden Aug 1913'.[2] She had already mentioned the novel in a letter to Berenson from Paris on 23 December 1912: 'It [a piece of gossip] is certainly full of "human interest", and what a document it's going to be for my next Op. – The Man of Genius!'[3]

Her letters to her publisher, Scribner's,[4] tell the story of her plans for the novel, its abandonment and the reasons for that abandonment. These reasons are significant to an understanding of her feelings about the place of a writer whose standards are those of an ordered society in a changed postwar world. She says in *A Backward Glance*:

It was growing more and more evident that the world I had grown up in and been formed by had been destroyed in 1914, and I felt myself incapable of transmuting raw material of the after-war world into a work of art. (*BG* 370)

The letters to Scribner's show the growth of this feeling, explain the radical changes to the novel which eventually resulted in *Hudson River Bracketed* and *The Gods Arrive* and indicate the length of time she worked on *Literature* after beginning it seriously in the summer of 1913 (which was as much a watershed in her own life as 1914 proved to be in Europe).[5]

Her first letter about *Literature* to Charles Scribner, written on 23 February 1914, tells him that it was to be a big book of about forty-five chapters – presumably she had by this time completed the chapter summaries – which it would take until January 1916 to complete: 'It is to be rather a full & leisurely account of a young man's life from his childhood to its end.'

But in a letter to Charles Scribner on 29 December 1914 she tells him that she has had to put the project aside owing to the outbreak of war. Her fuller explanation for this follows on 30 January 1915:

> I am beginning now to want to get back to work, and am kept back only by the steady drudge of the charities in which, like everyone else here, I am involved. At first I could not *write*, and it was maddening to think I could have made a little money for the charities I wanted so much to help, and yet to be so absolutely pen-tied.

In the spring of the following year, 30 March 1916, she procrastinates further – uncharacteristically, for she had always previously completed her planned works for Scribner: 'I have every hope of finishing *Literature* after the war, but it is on too large a scale to be taken up now. What I am doing is much slighter' (i.e. *Glimpses of the Moon*).

Two years later, in the spring of 1918, Edith Wharton and Charles Scribner exchange sharp letters on the subject of Literature. She writes on 13 April:

> In your letter you ask why I have not offered you a novel for a long time. You do not, I suppose, mean for publication in Scribner's, as I have offered you *two*, since the war, to replace 'Literature', the subject of which it was really impossible to treat, with the world crashing around one. I offered you 'Summer' & you said you preferred to wait for 'Literature', and then I suggested another, which I have never finished.

Charles Scribner replies on 6 May 1918:

> My understanding was that we had definitely engaged 'Literature' as a serial and there was no question of 'replacing' it with another, but pending its completion, which was delayed and for how long I did not realize, you suggested that we use another which you appeared to regard as a less important story.

Edith Wharton repeats the point she made in April with more emphasis on 23 May:

> I think you will find in referring to my letters that I said it might be difficult to write 'Literature' after the war, for the simple reason that these four years have so much changed the whole aspect of life that it is not easy to say now that one's literary tendencies will be when the war is over.

In the above letter she appears to realize that the war is going to prove more than a temporary interruption to her work, although she seems to hope still that she will complete *Literature*:

> I am doing my best to function literarily, being indeed a-thirst for my own job. But it is a good deal like writing a novel while balanced on a tight-rope to attempt portraying this convulsed world. That is why I have given up 'Literature' temporarily, though I like it best of my données, and hope to get back to it when the air clears. At present writing is next to impossible.[6]

But on 12 September 1919 she admits to Charles Scribner that 'Literature' in its original form seems outdated:

> In the first relief from war anxieties I thought it might be possible to shake off the question which is tormenting all novelists at present: 'Did the adventures related in this book happen before the war or did they happen since?' With the resulting difficulty that, if they happened before the war, I seem to have forgotten how people felt, and what their point of view was. I should feel ashamed of these hesitations if I did not find that all novelists I know are much in the same predicament. Perhaps it will not last much longer and we shall be able to get back some sort of perspective, but at present, between the objection of the public to the so-called war stories and the difficulty of the author to send his imagination backward, the situation is a bewildering one. As you know, I several times, during the war, offered to replace 'Literature' by other novels, which did not involve the study of such complex social conditions and dealt with people less affected by the war. As you preferred to wait for 'Literature' these two other tales, 'Summer' and 'The Marne', were given to other magazines, and I continued to hope that I should see my way to going on with 'Literature'.

In April 1921, in a letter to W.C. Brownell, she is still hoping:

> The war dealt that masterpiece a terrible blow. I still 'carry' it about with me, and long to make it the dizzy pinnacle of my work; but *when* did it all happen? And what repercussion did 1914–1920 have in my young man? I wrote Mr Scribner early in the war, and offered him several

'Ersatzes', among them 'Summer' and 'The Marne', but he preferred to wait. I don't yet despair of situating the tale; but there isn't enough perspective yet.

It would to be a reasonable assumption from these letters – and from the appearance of the manuscripts – that she worked steadily on 'Literature' during the second half of 1913 until her war work began to take priority in 1914. The drafts under discussion in this chapter appear to date from that period with few, if any, later additions. From these letters it is seen that the subject remained close to her heart over a long time, from at least 1912 until the publication of *Hudson River Bracketed* and *The Gods Arrive* in 1929 and 1932 respectively.

After the date on the flyleaf of the notebook comes a list of characters' names. Edith Wharton asserts in *A Backward Glance* that:

> My characters always appear with their names . . . Any character I unchristened instantly died on my hands. Only gradually, and in a very few cases, have I gained enough mastery over my creatures to be able to effect the change . . . a still more spectral element in my creative life is the sudden appearance of names without characters. (*BG* 201)

Blake Nevius suggests that she was influenced in her ideas on the subject of characters' names by James's Preface to *The Portrait of a Lady*[7] but not in her practice. The fact that the list of names appears at the beginning of her notebook certainly indicates that Edith Wharton thought names important, probably that names preceded situation, possibly that this was her usual way of beginning a novel. Unquestionably it can be seen that the names of her characters are not as immutable as she declares.[8]

To have caught Edith Wharton out in, at worst, an exaggeration does not invalidate entirely her view of her method of constructing a novel – especially on the basis of this one unpublished work – but we are entitled to be suspicious of her assertions and to challenge them by comparison with her actual practice. But more important is to discover what that method was and whether it achieves her stated imperative of verisimilitude.

With characters' names – and naming is, after all, the simplest form of characterization – verisimilitude demands probability and suitability. Despite Edith Wharton's stress on names as an integral part of the character, the names of her characters, particularly those from the Midwest of America, often appear satirical and therefore an authorial imposition. Bowler Bush and Carmen Bliss are examples from *Literature*. Richard Thaxter, the artist–hero of *Literature*, appears with his credible name from the first page of the notebook:

but the hero of *Hudson River Bracketed* and *The Gods Arrive* is
saddled with the Christian name Advance, after the Midwest town
where his father made great material advance through real estate.
While clearly this name is satirical – Edith Wharton is mocking a
society which sees progress in terms of wealth and change and scorns
anything not new – it takes on an ironic aspect as the novel
progresses and Vance is seen to advance by going back to the past and
traditional forms. In this case, the name is suitable and even probable
for an American, however unlikely it may sound to Europeans. When
Bernard Berenson remonstrates with her over the implausibility of
the names Undine Spragge and Indiana Frisk in *The Custom of
the Country*, she replies that life is stranger than fiction: 'Naïf
enfant. And how about Lurline Spreckels . . . & Florida Yurlee, two
'actualités' who occur to me instantly? As for similar instances the
'Herald' register will give you a dozen any morning.'[9]

Berenson might have replied that fiction as defined by Edith
Wharton has an obligation to be convincing which real life is not. A
stronger defence would have been that unbelievable names do not
necessarily mean unbelievable characters: as she says in *The Writing
of Fiction*: 'Captain Deucace and Rev. Mr. Quiverful are alive
enough.' She admits in *A Backward Glance*, when discussing the
appearance of her characters complete with names, that 'sometimes
these names seem to me affected, sometimes almost ridiculous: but I
am obliged to own that they are never fundamentally unsuitable' (*BG*
201). The very oddness of the names of fictional characters seems to
her to be a guarantee of authenticity:

> When in a book by someone else I meet people called by current names I
> always say to myself: 'Ah, those names were tied on afterwards', and I
> often find that the characters thus labelled are less living than the others.
> (*BG* 201)

Judging from *Literature* and the two later novels with a novelist
as the hero, the names of the characters where improbably are
appropriate – for example, Carmen Bliss the sexual temptress in
Literature and Floss Delaney who plays a similar role in the later
novels – but their very aptness makes them unreal: the names seem
suspiciously like those of the 'types' of early fiction. Characters may
come alive despite their names but, especially in the case of Vance
Weston, contrivance can be distracting.

The notebooks for *Literature* offer a valuable insight into Edith
Wharton's method of creating characters. Although the characters
did not 'appear' in quite such complete form as she declares in her
autobiography, the central character, at least, she seems to know as if

he were whole from the beginning, even at the note stage, for she gives his thoughts and opinions rather than beginning from the outside with physical description. Nevertheless, the man of genius as a type precedes the birth of Richard Thaxter, as can be seen from the page gummed into the notebook and the letter to Berenson. Once the type has become the individual, the other characters grow around this central character. They are rarely described other than through Dick's eyes or in relation to him, and the ideas for plot and scenes revolve around him and his development as a writer.

The distractions of the external world are symbolized by two women – as they are by two similar women in the Vance Weston novels – the one appealing to the hero's mind, the other to his body. Rose, who even in these brief notes can be seen as intellectual and sensitive, is described through thoughts and emotions, either her own or Dick's toward her: 'Rose Ledwith has the hyper sensibility, the over-exquisiteness of perception, the too-prompt "emotivity" – wh. are apt to be found with a certain kind of distinguished talent.' Carmen Bliss is, appropriately, only described in physical terms, apart from a line of dialogue through which she reveals her frivolity: 'Carmen says: "I don't see why Paul thinks I'm extravagant. I'm wearing last year's sables." ' That Edith Wharton sees these two characters as contrasting types rather than individuals is clear from two notes near the beginning of the notebook:

Rose
Now and then he saw the buried cities in her eyes.

Carmen
She had crescent-shaped eyes – the lower lids curving slightly upward, & the corners of the upper drooping over it, & giving her an odd exotic look, as though she saw blue temples on yellow rivers.

These characters were created to provide elements surrounding the hero, to fulfil roles, and, because from their conception they are one-sided, Edith Wharton has difficulty in making them 'live'.

The other types who are later present in the Vance Weston novels and exist in these early notes are the Patron and the Sage. The characters, like the sex, of the patron changes, but that of the sage, Levick in *Literature*, Frenside in the later novels, remains constant throughout the novel's evolution as a mouthpiece for Edith Wharton's ideas on life and art. It is to this character in the notebook that the aphorisms, in the recognizably acid tone of its creator, are attached. For example: 'Levick says: – What an appalling thing literature has become now clergymen's daughters have taken to writing about fauns'; 'The measure of a character is in the nature of its dislikes'; 'The

worst thing about women is that if a man doesn't go on being in love
with them forever they always think he never was from the beginning.'
Being a type, a megaphone, and speaking in aphorisms, this character
has obstacles to overcome in becoming convincingly lifelike.

The central cast of characters for *Literature* through to *The Gods
Arrive* is established as early as the notebook: the writer–hero is
surrounded by parents and relations, the teacher–sage, the patron,
the sensual woman, the spiritual woman and the helpless woman. The
character of the hero possesses not only experiences in common with
his creator but also the dual nature with its desire for order in life and
art based on traditional values and its impulse towards individual
imagination which sets it apart. Through her hero, Dicky to Vance,
Edith Wharton asserts her belief in classical principles and portrays a
romantic conception of the artist as someone unique firstly in his
ability to turn experience, even suffering, into art, and secondly, to
enter so completely into other people's lives that he loses his own
identity. Edith Wharton retains this idea of the writer, the 'man of
genius', and the surrounding cast for two decades partly because the
early stages of *Literature* (including a scenario and chapter summaries
of the entire novel) and nine chapters were completed before the war
took priority. This careful and ordered approach enables her to
reassemble the basic ingredients for *Hudson River Bracketed* and *The
Gods Arrive*, the novels which encapsulate the classical ideals and the
romantic responses which, as has been seen, run through her work
from *The Decoration of Houses*.

At the back of the small notebook, Edith Wharton wrote what she
called a 'scenario' for the novel now entitled *Literature* rather than, as
on the front cover, *Man of Genius*. The assumption must be that she
wrote this scenario (Appendix II) before she planned the chapter
summaries which come half-way through the notebook. The most
distinctive quality of the nineteen pages comprising the scenario is the
fluency with which they are written; there are few corrections and the
appearance of the handwriting suggests that it was written at one
sitting for it shows little sign of hesitation, the same ink is used
throughout, and the writing becomes progressively less neat as if her
hand grew tired. (A comparison of pages two and three with pages
eighteen and nineteen included at the beginning of Appendix II
demonstrates this point.) But if the appearance of the manuscript
suggests that she wrote it quickly, the content indicates that it was the
result of a period of contemplation, of 'brooding', on her original
ideas and initial notes during which the cast of characters take on
roles, and episodes in the hero's life evolve.

The chapter summaries, which come about half-way through the
notebook, show that Edith Wharton intended the novel to consist of

forty-two chapters divided into seven books (Appendix III), nine chapters of which she completed. The material of the scenario is ordered and shaped to mark the progress of the hero from childhood to death, with his age carefully noted beside the chapters at intervals, and the emphasis is on his external life rather than his inner development. As with the scenario, it appears from the manuscript that the summaries were written at one sitting.

There are few important changes made between the scenario and the chapter summaries.[10] The following example of the way in which she builds up a scene from a brief note shows how details of plot, character and motive are added and by the chapter summary stage seeds of future action and development have been sown:

(1) *Notes*: In his liaison with Mrs R [sic] they take every risk, and are never found out; till it is all over, & he is giving her a last kiss, perfunctory on his side, resigned on hers – when the husband comes in –

(2) *Scenario*: Play total failure. Dick learns almost same time his own money almost gone, & is confronted by obligation to repay Cleaver. In talk, the latter lets slip that not he but his sister, Mrs Spofford Birnam (a good deal older) has 'put up' the money. Dick, aghast, goes to tell her of his difficulty & to thank her. – The scene, to his dismay, turns to sentiment, & he doesn't know how to escape. Brief liaison, wh. he tries to save from grotesqueness by poetizing it – but she is a 'pseudo-cult figure' and bores him, & is jealous & silly, & finally reminds him of his debt – & it is all sordid and shabby. At length she grows ashamed of the part she has played, & (his mother dying – or perhaps Grandma B?) he repays the money, & they are having a quiet scene of goodbye, that seems to retrieve the meanness of the episode – when, just as Dick is kissing her before leaving, Spofford Birnam comes in and 'surprises' them.

(3) *Chapter summaries*: Chap IX Production. Total failure. Despair. How shall he pay? Discovers that Mrs Birnam has advanced the money, not Cleaver. Goes to thank her. Sentimental scene. He is in the toils. Chap X The first 'love-affair'. Dick's misery. The pseudo-culture of Mrs Birnam's set. His longing to get away from it all. He runs across Rose Chancellor every now & then – also Levick, whose talk makes him more & more sick of the people he is seeing & the life he is leading. Chap XI He is doing hack journalism (literary criticisms etc) to try to pay off Mrs B. – He is thrown (in her group) with Edwin Silmore, the Prophet of the pseudos – a rich & kindly ass who takes a great fancy to Dick. Chap XII Meanwhile the Birnam bondage grows daily more intolerable. Quarrels, jealousy of Mrs B. (15 years older). Dick rebellious and bitter. At length Mrs B. grows ashamed of the part she has played, & – Grandma Boole having died about this time and left her grandson a legacy – Dick is suddenly able to pay his debt. The fact softens him, but he is as firmly resolved as ever to be free. Mrs B. understands & accepts this, & they say goodbye. As they are exchanging a last perfunctory kiss Birnam comes in & 'surprises' them.

For a final version of this scene we have to look to *Hudson River Bracketed* because the second draft of *Literature* breaks off just before the point where it was planned to take place. The scenes between Vance Weston and Jet Pulsifer in Chapters 26 and 27 of *Hudson River Bracketed* clearly originate in the projected scene between Dick and Mrs Birnam although the balance of the relationship is different: Dick is forced into a liaison because the older woman is discovered to be his benefactor; Vance might have benefited by receiving a prize for literature if he had not rejected her advances – 'had he imprisoned her hand the prize would have been his' – and later asked her for a loan – 'if you really believe in me, will you lend me two thousand dollars?' He finally seals his fate by revealing that not only is he married but also loves his wife.

Between the notes and the scenario of *Literature* it is the formative events in the hero's life that are filled in rather than details of his inner world or of his creative life. The satellite characters are developed within their limited roles encircling the hero. For example, in Book I Dick's father, a clergyman with 'doubts', is seen by Dick as a superior character, and his mother as a hypocrite from a family 'of those worldly experiences he [the father], a shy unworldly person, stood somewhat in awe' – quite wrongly as Dick discovers after his father's death for his two uncles are incompetent to the point of dishonesty. The character of his father has clearly been already more fully developed than it is in the scenario, for there is a note: 'First chapter already written' and the chapter summaries confirm that the first chapters had already been written to contain the hero's early impressions and home influences including that of his father. All the characters, apart from the father, represent love or money or both and are seen as obstacles rather than benefactors even when they begin by helping. For example, Edwin Silmore, the patron, 'a dilettantish person', sends Dick to Europe to travel, study and write a "great book", but when he returns having written nothing and without any ideas Silmore does not understand and becomes cold. Levick, the sage, a 'genius without creative faculty', who has been Dick's 'greatest source of strength' becomes jealous 'not of his temporary success but of his really great achievement' and as a result tells Dick's wife when his affair with Carmen Bliss flares up again. Even Rose, as self-sacrificing and stoical as Halo in the later novels, becomes a burden and 'drives him wild' although he does return to her at the end when ill and lacking in inspiration.

The subsidiary characters are seen in the notes, scenario and chapter summaries to provide essential experiences and also distraction for the hero: in addition they function to show him as unique, a man of genius, by providing ordinary reactions and emotions in contrast with his special, creative nature. For example, Dick finds relief from suffering in writing in contrast with Rose: 'She spends in feeling (aesthetically and emotionally) what he finds full outlet for in expression. . . . Genius is the greatest dérivatif of life – the only thing that saves one from the horrors of being intelligent.'

This note develops in the scenario and chapter summaries into the incident where Dick leaves Rose over their quarrel about his return to Carmen Bliss and he 'decides to kill himself, & at that moment the thought of a big book comes to him, & he sits down & writes the scenario'. Rose suffers, 'forgives and pities'. In *The Gods Arrive*, Halo Tarrant, left alone by Vance Weston for months without any communication, discovers from a newspaper that he has been seeing Floss Delaney again and remembers and rereads the story the young Vance had written about his pain over Floss's betrayal years before:

> He had suffered thus agonizingly – as she was suffering now – but by pouring his suffering into a story he had been able to cleanse his soul of it. Ah, happy artists! No wonder they were careless of other people's wounds when they were born with the power to heal their own so easily . . . (*GA* 329)

Although Dick and Vance need the experiences and suffering that the other characters provide – Dick thinks of himself as 'an instrument' vibrating to outside influence and Vance feels 'as if his art must be fed by suffering, like some exquisite insatiable animal' (*HB* 392) – they also afford distractions. Dick is able to write 'in his misery when his unhappy love obscures his art'; Vance 'knew that Laura Lou, the inspirer of this desire [to write a poem], was also the insuperable obstacle to its fulfilment' (*HB* 184). The contrast between the woman who loves him and the hero, between the ordinary person and the artist, is further shown in the desire of the former to be with the loved one and the need of the latter to be alone. Dick feels that he needs solitude to experience 'that sense of power which comes in long vigils, & in ardent incommunicable hours'; Vance 'was beginning to discover that he no longer need a companion in these explorations of the depths; what he most wanted then was to be alone' (*GA* 79). From the chapter summaries it can be seen that Edith Wharton planned for Dick just such an escape to write an important book as Vance achieves toward the end of *The Gods Arrive*:

> Furious and disgusted with his sentimental dilemma [Dick] flies both women & goes off to the wilds. He does not let Rose know where he is. In a fury of inspiration he sets to work on his third book, which is to be the greatest. He feels himself in full command of his genius. (LIT Ch. summaries, Ch. XXXVI, Book VI)

But this romantic picture of the artist as a man set apart by reason of his nature – Vance wonders 'if the creator of imaginary beings must always feel alone among the real ones' – and of his needs, is balanced by the picture of him as one who also particularly needs an ordered life and the stability of a secure income.

The cast of minor characters outlined in the notes for *Literature* and finally developed in the Vance Weston novels provide or deny these necessities as well as emotional experiences for the hero. From the scenario and chapter summaries of the early novel it can be seen that Edith Wharton puts financial considerations at the centre of life for the artist as much as for all her central characters. In none of her fiction does she fail to particularize the financial status of her characters nor to emphasize the importance of money in their destinies; her artist heroes, however romantic her conception of their unique qualities which set them apart, are never seen as being above everyday practical anxieties. Richard Thaxter and Vance Weston, no less than Lily Bart or Sophy Viner, are affected by lack of money. The characters upon whom Dick depends for money, or who are responsible for his lack of it, clearly influence the course of his life – and these characters reappear in a more developed form in the published novels. Vance Weston's problems with money are less easily solved than Dick's and more obstructive, but the pattern of their difficulties and their solution is the same and neither has any compunction in accepting money in order to indulge a need to travel and write.

In the scenario and chapter summaries for *Literature* the implicit concern is with the plot; minor characters are not developed but are seen as catalytic agents in the life of the hero. Edith Wharton is revealed as a careful planner and the structure of the novel is clearly seen to be that of the *Künstlerroman* in which each episode functions to reveal something about the artist–hero, or to open or close certain possibilities for him. The succession of episodes which she outlines run thus: Dick's father dies leaving inefficient uncles in charge of Dick's money; the money dwindles and Dick therefore accepts Cleaver's money for the production of his play; the play fails and he discovers that the money was Mrs Birnham's, which leads him into a liaison with her; this is discovered by her husband so Dick accepts Silmore's offer of funds to escape to Europe; in Europe he meets Rose again; when he returns to America without the expected novel, his patron, Silmore, rejects him and he becomes a journalist to earn his living and publishes Rose's stories, which leads to their marriage when he becomes editor with a respectable salary; he leaves the paper to write a novel which is a success so he returns to Europe where he meets again Carmen Bliss to whom he had been introduced on the

previous trip by a childhood friend; he only returns to America and
Rose when Carmen, now a Princess, drops him; Rose knows about
the affair but they adjust and Dick, after a struggle, completes a novel
so good that it arouses the jealousy of his long-time mentor, Levick;
although Dick and Rose are now happier, he succumbs to Carmen
when she turns up in New York and cultivates Dick now that he is a
celebrity; Levick, out of spite, tells Rose, who reproaches Dick which
sends him first back to Carmen and then, to escape both women, to
the wilds where he writes furiously; on the failure of his inspiration,
Dick returns to Rose who realizes he is ill and, when the repentant
Levick gives them money, they go to the Mediterranean where they
are happy, Dick starts writing again but dies before finishing the
book. Rose, their son, Dick's novel and Rose and Levick's biography
are left to continue the story of the artist.

The chronological plan of the novel outlined here did not, of
course, limit the narration to a chronological perspective. Edith
Wharton begins the novel from a narrative standpoint after the end of
the action, which focuses attention less on what happens to her hero
and more on why and how it happens, less on plot and more on
character: 'The most decisive event of Richard Thaxter's life –
though one unrecorded in his wife's admirably compiled Biography
– occurred on a hot June Sunday in his father's church at Tryan-on-
Hudson.' At the same time, her use of the adjective 'most decisive'
shows that the events to be related will be seen to be casual. Edith
Wharton felt that, as well as illustrating character, each episode
should present options to a character from which he must appear to
be free to make a choice. The novelist must;

> Above all, bear in mind at each step that his business is not to ask what
> the situation would be likely to make of his characters, but what his
> characters, being what they are, would make of the situation. (*WF* 140)

The sense of inevitability must come from the characters rather than
from the action. The scenario for *Literature* affords an example: the
failure of Dick's play leaves him vulnerable to the overtures of Mrs
Birnham and Silmore; he has a choice, and the choice he makes
illustrates his character as well as, in retrospect, seeming inevitable
given his personality. He might have resisted Mrs Birnham's advance
– as Vance does Mrs Pulsifier's – or refused Silmore's money, but he
succumbs to both temptations.

The scenario and chapter summaries outline the influences on the
writer as a man of live and money and external events; it is not until
the first draft of *Literature* that the influences on him as an artist
of spoken language and literature, on which there are notes, are

developed. The skeleton of the novel, carefully constructed in the early stages contained in the notebook, show Edith Wharton to be a meticulous craftswoman, despite her assertion that she let her 'tales shape themselves into obedience to their inner organism', and this skeleton gives her a firm structure on which to build character and scenes.

'Nothing shows the quality of the novelist's imagination more clearly than the incidents he singles out to illuminate the course of events and the inner workings of his people's souls': in the scenario Edith Wharton singles out scenes for later development. To follow these 'illuminating incidents', the importance of which she emphasizes in *The Writing of Fiction*, from the brief outline in the scenario through to the final version of *Literature*, elucidates her method as a novelist and defines her comments in *The Writing of Fiction*. One of the most important functions of her careful planning appears to be to select and place scenes to give them the greatest significance and dramatic effect. Of the episodes outlined in the notebook, only six are dramatized in the uncompleted final draft. Of these, two are scenes in Dick's childhood, which will be discussed later, and one, which takes place at the beginning of Book Two, shows Dick's novel being read aloud when he realizes his power with words, has significant encounters, and possibilities are opened up for him. (Part of this scene is used to show the extent and type of her corrections: see Appendix VII). The other three scenes are a sequence where in the last the hero sees and understands the two earlier scenes more clearly and this revelation marks a watershed in his life.

These three scenes (with a fourth seen through Dick's memory, but not outlined in the early stages) are concerned with Dick's clergyman father's 'doubts' and his mother's hypocrisy and deception. They are sketched in the scenario like this:

> Scene during his father's illness, when Mr Thaxter tries to tell him that he has never 'believed', & Mrs Thaxter, gathering up all her courage, says: 'Your father is delirious', & puts Dick out of the room.

> A few days later, edifying death-bed scene, Mr Thaxter scarcely conscious, clergyman praying, Mrs Thaxter reading psalms, Dick brought in – & sees his father die in an odour of orthodoxy.

> (Several years afterward he taxes his mother with this, & she, though sincerely believing in the death-bed scene, *which she had got up herself*, nevertheless admits with tears that there were times when her husband 'had doubts.')

> Mr Thaxter's library: little theology, & no speculative or scientific books: Dick now understands why. His father was afraid, & tried to shut his eyes & stop his ears, & 'do his duty as a parish priest'.

In the final draft, the scene where Dick's father tries to confess his
lack of belief is preceded by a scene remembered by the boy as he
journeys through the snow from school to his father's bedside.
Although ostensibly a flashback in the mind of the child, the scene is
described in adult language and, occasionally, from an adult's viewpoint. The scene begins with a discussion about Dick's confirmation
between his father and a visiting cleric, Dr Lafford, 'greatly esteemed
for the eloquence of his sermons and the humour of his after-dinner
stories', which leads on to a scene between Dick and his father in
which the boy asks for an explanation of confirmation and 'the
mysteries of the Christian faith'. Mr Thaxter evades the questions
with: 'Ah, my boy – ah, my boy!' The scene is rounded off by a
comment on it made through the child's mind and conveyed by an
image which is picked up in the final scene of the sequence:

> The very note of Mr Thaxter's voice came back to Dick – its strange
> mingling of irony and sadness. He had not understood then; he did not
> understand now; but for an instant his face was swept by the cold fog that
> always hung about his father. (Notebook)

The significance of Mr Thaxter's evasions, remembered by Dick,
becomes clearer to the reader and to some extent to the boy when,
having arrived home, he is urged by his dying father to 'keep free'; his
father says:

> Listen. Don't be confirmed . . . wait . . . I made a terrible mistake . . . I
> entered the Church in ignorance . . . I hadn't studied . . . in the modern
> sense. Afterwards I woke up to things . . . to what the world's doing and
> thinking. You're too young to understand . . . but I couldn't free myself
> . . . Once you're in you're like a fly in a bottle . . . and your mother could
> never see – it would have killed her . . . (ibid.)

In bed that night Dick reflects on this 'confession' scene and
remembers his mother's anger when she interrupts them and 'it was
perfectly clear to Dick that his father had been watching for a
moment alone with him to entreat him to renounce Christianity'. The
implications for the child are terrifying:

> The possibility of his father dying, which had seemed the most dreadful
> thing conceivable, was as nothing compared to the thought of his lying
> close by in the darkness, defying the God of those black and sparkling
> abysses. (ibid.)

By linking the central 'confession' scene, planned in the scenario,
with an earlier scene retained and recollected in detail by the boy, and

by describing his thoughts and conclusions after it had taken place, Edith Wharton makes that central scene momentous in its effect on the hero and marks a stage in the growth of his understanding and development. This scene and the boy's reflections on it highlight the ironies and hypocrisies which underlie the deathbed scene which follows shortly. The clergyman who had urged Dick's confirmation and precipitated the first of Dick's discussions with his father about religion is called in by Dick's mother to force last communion on the dying man whose last words to his son are: 'This is peace.'

In the final scene of the sequence between Dick and his mother some years later, when she admits under pressure that her husband had had 'doubts', much that had been incomprehensible to the boy becomes clear to the young man and he learns from those previous scenes as well as the present one. This scene follows in full as it stands in the final draft of the novel, with all Edith Wharton's corrections in longhand incorporated.

The next morning he borrowed the housemaid's ladder, and began the attack. He had just effected a breach in a wall of black sermons, and was in the act of rescuing from behind it some imprisoned volumes on which he had detected the names of Spencer, Tyndall, Huxley, Helmholtz and Clifford, when he heard his mother's voice beneath him.

'Dick! What are you looking for?' She spoke with an authority that carried him back to the days before his father's death. But now he was a bigger boy.

'Nothing in particular. I just thought I'd like to go through father's books.'

She hesitated, 'I'm not sure your father would have wanted you to – yet.'

He squatted down on the ladder and faced her. 'Why?'

'Well . . . You're hardly old enough . . . There are books one oughtn't to read till one knows enough to understand them.'

'How can I tell if I can understand them till I've tried?'

'You might *think* you did – and then later you'd find they'd led you into all sorts of mistakes that you would have been spared if you'd been less ignorant.'

Dick did not consider the contingency worth discussing. 'I mean to know everything,' he simply stated.

His mother ignored this. 'There were certain books that even your father thought it better not to read, because he found they had a bad influence on him – I mean intellectually. That's why he put them away behind the others.' She held out her hand. 'Let me see the one you've taken out.'

Reluctantly he proferred it. 'Spencer. "First Principles" I shouldn't think there could be anything wrong with that. But it's so hard to tell. And it was at the back of the shelf. Oh, Dick, it may be unsettling!' She kept the book in her hand.

'What's unsettling?'

He knew she hated to be asked meanings, but he didn't care. She lowered her voice to say: 'Unchristian.'

The kind of books Mr Closser read?'

She nodded. 'You know he's most unhappy. He had to take a place in a steam-boat office, on a wretched salary, and he's married a horrid woman whom his mother can't receive.' She added firmly: 'Come down, Dick. I want you to respect your father's wishes.'

Dick obeyed – but her last words had given him his cue and he faced her stubbornly.

'Father's wish was that I should know things.'

'Whatever it was right for you to know.'

'I don't mean that. The day he was so ill, when I was along with him . . .'

His mother stood silent, uneasily fluttering the pages of the forbidden book.

'Didn't father ever have doubts – like Mr Closser?'

'Richard! Richard!'

'Then why was he afraid of unchristian books – if he was a Christian?'

'I didn't say he was afraid. I –'

'Yes you did. And why did he put them up here out of reach, if he wasn't?'

His mother murmured: 'I sometimes think you say things just to torture me!'

Dick's heart was beating high. 'You know I don't. But I don't understand . . . Father *wanted* me to know, and you say . . .'

'I say your father was wrong . . . wrong and wicked!'

'Father?' It burst from Dick in a cry. He looked long and steadily at his mother. 'Then that day – he wasn't delirious?'

She dropped the book and broke into tears. But he stood his ground, hardening with horror. She had deceived him then – his own mother! 'Father *did* want me to read things – he did!'

She sobbed silently, her black-edged handkerchief against her eyes. At length she controlled herself and said: 'He read too much – when he was young. Afterward . . . You see he put the books out of reach . . . And the day he died – have you forgotten?'

Dick looked at her doggedly: his heart was wrung, but not as she had meant to wring it. 'He *wanted* me to read things,' he repeated, as though the words possessed a mystic potency.

His mother laid her hand on his arm. 'But if I want you not to – yet? Won't you promise me to wait till college?'

He considered her compassionately but calmly. He was very sorry, with a sense of protection in his pity; he would have done anything in the world for her except the one thing she asked – that he should renounce the freedom his father had given him.

'I'm sorry mother, I don't see why I should.'

'Oh, you've no heart!' she murmured, turning abruptly from the room.

Left alone, Dick felt a pang of compunction. He hated to make his mother cry: he wished it could have been avoided. But she had not been fair to him; she had tried to mislead him with respect to his father's wishes. The thought, while it laid a heavy burden on his heart, steeled him in the determination to carry out his purpose. 'I must know all he wanted me to know' – it became almost a sacred obligation; and mounting the ladder he went on with his investigations. (Dr 2.)

From the outline in the scenario it appears that Edith Wharton intended to emphasize the mother's hypocrisy and self-delusion, but in the final version the emphasis is on intellectual freedom. Dick's father yearned for freedom from the orthodoxy to which he was committed as a clergyman; having failed to free himself he succeeds, posthumously, in showing his son the way to liberate himself from the confines of a narrow background by exploring a wider intellectual world through books. In the same way Edith Wharton herself had broken free from the restricted outlook and expectations of her society through the medium of her father's 'gentleman's library' – and Vance Weston sitting in the library at 'The Willows' begins his journey away from his limited philistine upbringing. The powerful image of the 'imprisoned books' guarded by 'black sermons' echoes the image used by Dick's father of himself as a 'fly in a bottle', a man trapped within out-of-date dogma while realizing that the fresh air of scientific philosophy existed outside. The images of cold and darkness in the earlier scenes and in the sick-room at the end similarly convey the picture of the unhappiness of a man alone with an insoluble problem, one which as perceived his young son 'hung between himself and the persons about him like one of those shifting sea-fogs that at one minute are just a chill in the air and the next a heavy curtain'.

This problem of a crisis of faith when faced with evolutionary theory and the concept of empirical knowledge – the subjects dealt with by the 'imprisoned books' – must certainly have seemed to Edith Wharton to belong to a different age when she returned to the novel after the First World War. She replaces this religious dilemma in *Hudson River Bracketed* with a preoccupation, satirically presented, with non-conformist sects. At the beginning of the book Vance invents a 'new religion':

He had been born into a world in which everything had been, or was being, renovated, and it struck him as an anomaly that all religions he had heard of had been in existence since he could remember; that is, at least sixteen years. (*HB* 7)

Towards the end of the book, Vance's grandmother, always naïvely enthusiastic about spiritual matters, turns up as a preacher in New

York bringing guidance to the 'Seekers' and Vance thinks back to his youthful invention, 'the creed whose originality had crumbled away with his first glimpse of the old philosophies' (*HRB* 328). Because the war had swept away the old values treasured by Edith Wharton, she dramatizes her belief in them by taking as her hero a young man from the Midwest where those values and all that embodied them had never existed and showing that he had to go back to the past before he could develop enough intellectually to be free. Dick Thaxter's progress towards intellectual freedom begins with his exploration of new ideas; Vance Weston's begins with his exploration of the accumulated wisdom of the past. 'What the world's doing and thinking' changed between 1913 and 1917 in such a way that, to Edith Wharton, what was new was rather to be scorned than explored: by the time she completed Vance Weston's story in the early 1930s the changes were even greater. In 'A Little Girl's New York' published in *Harper's Magazine* in 1938 she writes:

> The succeeding years have witnessed such convulsions, social and political that those earlier disturbances now seem no more than a premonitory tremor; and the changes between the customs of my youth and the world of even ten years ago a mere crack in the ground compared with the chasm now dividing the world from the present one.

In this same articles Edith Wharton recounts briefly the experience in her childhood on which she based a significant event in Dick's life, which, together with the incident of a childish kiss with which she opens *A Backward Glance*, affords a useful example of the way in which she transmutes reality into fiction. In 'A Little Girl's New York' she recounts how she and her father regularly used to attend their parish church for the sake of hearing the Reverend Dr Washburn, 'a man of great learning, and possessed of a singularly beautiful voice':

> It is to Dr. Washburn that I owe the discovery of the matchless beauty of English seventeenth century prose; and the organ-roll of Isaiah, Job and above all, of the lament of David over the dead Absalom, always come back to me in the accents of that voice, of which I can only say that it was worthy to interpret the English Bible.

In *Literature* this memory becomes a fully dramatized scene which opens the novel and is introduced in the opening sentence as: 'The most decisive event in Richard Thaxter's life'.

The passages of description which introduce this event evoke the feelings of a seven-year-old child in church with the clarity and sympathy of a personal memory but also introduce the situation of this fictional child, Richard Thaxter: the smells and feeling of 'drowsy ecstasy' appear to belong to the author's childhood whereas the embarrassment of looking at a father's 'fussy white presence' as officiating cleric belongs entirely to her invented character. The decisive event, 'which even there, on the spot, he obscurely felt to be a great event, an event as great as could happen in anything so small as his life', is to hear his father from the pulpit recite David's lament: 'O my son Absalom, my son, my son Absalom, would God I had died for thee, O Absalom, my son, my son'

> That was what happened – this rain of celestial syllables pouring down on him from heights higher than the swallow's nest and the summer sky . . . But he didn't care a straw what the words meant: that had nothing to do with it. He simply noticed that they *were* words; and that was the great event. He had noticed many things already; birds, dogs, beetles, tadpoles, people's faces, the look of rooms and the pictures on their walls. But he had never noticed words, or the sound of words joined together; and now the wonder of the linked syllables seemed to catch his little heart in a grasp of fire. (*LIT* Dr 2 p.2)

In *A Backward Glance* she says that in early childhood:

> My imagination lay there, coiled and sleeping, a mute hibernating creature, and at the least touch of common things – flowers, animals, words, especially the sound of words, apart from their meaning – it already stirred in its sleep. (*BG* 4)

Edith Wharton uses her memory of the earliest signs of her vocation as a writer in her portrayal of her writer–hero and develops and emphasizes its significance by showing the little boy after his experience in church longing to ask 'where his wonderful words came from and why they were so wonderful' but being misunderstood, misconstrued by his obtuse relatives. These characters, while not portraits of real characters, are clearly grounded in the stifling society in which she was brought up, the 'little world' with its 'hoard of petty maxims with which its elders preached down every sort of initiative'. They are presented through the eyes of the small boy and, at the same time, ironically by the author: Uncle Wayne was 'a great reader (one had Aunt Lucy's word for it) and quoted poetry now and then, to the visible admiration of everyone but Dicky's father'; Uncle Horace knew 'more than the gardener, the coachman, the stable-boy or Bowler Bush, the sexton's son (a mine of wisdom) put together'; Aunt Elizabeth, mainly seen as an embodiment of a 'complicated series of taboos', nevertheless was 'not unlettered' for she possessed 'rows and rows of sermons bound in black cloth' and 'Letters of clergymen who had died young, and Memorials of ladies in white caps' and Dicky occasionally 'had seen her reading a volume of the cultivation of small fruits or A Lady's Guide to Lace-making'. The descriptions end with the ironic comment: 'It will be seen that the group around the Rectory table was one that ought to have been able to answer any question a little boy might put.'

Dick is restrained from putting his question not by any intuition of the limitations of the adults but mainly by the fear 'if he mentioned anything connected with "church", of raising the vexed question of Sunday School.' He decided prudently not to ask about the words he had heard his father speak from the pulpit.

On the table, Dicky had the luck to find a stray sheet of note-paper, and – rarer still – a pencil; and prone on the floor he began to write. The magic words still sang through his be-puddinged brain and his impulse was to give them shape. But this was not easy. Slowing printing each letter, he laboured on with frowning forehead and restless heels; but though the words were so clear inside his head they grew indistinct when he tried to put them down.

'Oh my so nabsalan my son my so nabsalan, wood god' (there were wood-gods in his fairy books, so he understood that) – at this point the reconstitution broke down: the next words sounded like 'died had died', but that didn't make sense, and he lay pondering.

'Hullo! Hullo! Writing a letter, young man?' Uncle Wayne's omniscient eye-glass bore down on him before he could shield the paper.

'No.'

'What is it, then? *Not doing lessons on Sunday, I hope?*' The clarion-note of reform rang out through Uncle Wayne's nose.

Mrs. Thaxter intervened. 'Perhaps it's a story. Dicky sometimes writes stories; don't you darling?'

Darling lay mute.

'Oho! Stories, indeed? We're going to be an author, are we? Is this a story?'

'No.'

'Dicky, don't answer in that way. Sit up and show Uncle Wayne what you've been writing.'

'Yes, do, dear,' murmured Grandma Boole, fumbling fondly for the spectacles in her velvet chatelaine-bag (Horace's last present from Paris).

The fat was in the fire, then – no help for it! Dicky pulled away his hand and sullenly surrendered what it hid. Uncle Wayne straightened the glasses on his inquisitive brown nose and read out: 'my so nabsalan – what on earth – "O wabsalan –" oh, of course; of course! *Absalom*. I see – I see.' He laughed ridiculously.

'Are you writing a story about Absalom, dearest?' Dicky's grandmother encouraged him.

'No.'

'What is it, then? It doesn't make sense,' said Uncle Wayne irritably.

'Yes, it does. Father said it?' *That* was irrefutable!

'Said it? When did he say it?' Again the idiot laugh!

'Dicky, *answer*,' his mother commanded.

'In church.'

Grandma Boole melted. 'I told you so, Margaret! I often see him listening. Is it father's sermon you're trying to write out, darling?'

'No.'

'What *is* it, then? George, do look!'

Her son-in-law, roused from one of his fits of abstraction (family parties often seemed to bring them on) strolled over to Mrs Boole and took the paper from her. He scanned it, smiled and gave it back to Dicky. 'David's lament – a phonetic version.' Mr. Thaxter wandered away again, and Dicky was perfectly aware that he was edging to the door with the design of slipping out unnoticed.

'Ah, ah, to be sure!' Uncle Wayne exclaimed. '"O Absalom, my son Absalom, my –" how does it go? Beautiful thing – "would to God that I had died for thee, O my son Absalom": yes, that's it.'

'Oh, *no*!' Dicky almost screamed. The misplaced syllables seemed to writhe with pain.

' "No" what?'

But he couldn't explain.

'A very beautiful passage – a celebrated passage,' Uncle Wayne continued. 'Of course, Dick, you know the story of David and Absalom?'

Dicky pondered, and once more said 'No'. What he wanted to explain – but again couldn't – was that at the moment it didn't matter in the least about the story . . . He looked from one to the other of the wise mysterious faces overhead and touched his paper. 'I want to know why it's *like that*.'

'You see he *longs* to be taught the Word of God!' his grandmother wailed. 'Sit down here, darling. Once, you see, King David, who was a very great and wise King –'

'No – no!' Dicky stamped. Here they were thrusting the 'story' at him again! 'I only want to know about – about the words themselves.'

'But the story tells about the words.'

He shook his head and pressed the paper close. Two tears gathered and dropped from his eyelashes. (*LIT* Dr 2)

Not only the central experience of this scene but also the lack of understanding and of writing materials were features of Edith Wharton's own childhood: her mother crushes her with an 'icy comment' at her first attempt at a novel, and she tells sadly that 'it was not thought necessary to feed my literary ambitions with foolscap'.

She objectifies her memories by creating characters to surround a hero distanced from herself by a difference of sex and she creates a fictional world unlike the one in which she was brought up in external details. In the passage quoted here she presents dramatically as a climax at the end of the first chapter the characters and their relationships previously described and the themes of the innate instincts of the writer and of religious hypocrisy and doubt outlined in the previous page. The comment and description interwoven with the dialogue control the reader's response to the characters, drawing him into a closer sympathy with the child than the narrative had done and distancing him from the crass grow-up. The scene is framed by Dick's angle of vision – for example, in the first two paragraphs, we know what he is trying to do and are told at intervals how he sees the adults and what he feels – but the author's comments explain and evaluate so that there is a double vision of the action and dialogue, the subjective 'going behind' into the mind of a participant and the objective view. For example: 'the omniscient eye-glass' and 'the clarion-call of reform' interpret the character of Uncle Wayne from a standpoint and in language extraneous to the child. This dual point of view interlaced with the dialogue creates a scene which illustrates the themes and characters and illuminates what has gone before as well as what is to come more effectively than a scene controlled purely by the child's consciousness could have done without disturbing the illusion that it is the hero's childish consciousness that is central.

The dialogue functions to reveal the characters and reinforce what has been told about them and fulfils, on the whole, the purposes that Edith Wharton lays down for it in *The Writing of Fiction*: that is, that it should be used sparingly for culminating moments to 'emphasize the crises of the tale', to enhance the passage of time and 'to gather up the loose strands of passion and emotion'. Furthermore it comes convincingly from the mouths of the characters – 'characters must talk as they would in reality' – and is significant and relevant to the tale. Possibly the scene is protracted beyond its significance to the novel as a whole and the fact that she did not include it in any form in the published novels suggest that she felt that it lacked relevance.

Dick's response to the sound of words is again dramatized in the following chapter after a description of 'the next most important event' in his life which is based on Edith Wharton's earliest memory, one by which she 'was wakened to conscious life by the two tremendous forces of love and vanity'. Dicky, while out walking with his father on a cold winter's day, meets a little girl with her grandfather and, while the adults talk above them, Dicky, fascinated by the red cheeks of the little girl behind her veil, plants a kiss: 'The white knitted veil over her face made her look like a Valentine – one of the expensive ones in layers. . . . Pushing back the veil he pressed a kiss on the scarlet cheek beneath' (*LIT* Dr 2).

Edith Wharton, throughout her life much occupied with dress, having described the bonnet she wore when out walking with her father, continues:

As the air was very cold a gossamer veil of the finest Shetland wool was
drawn about the bonnet and hung down over the wearer's round red
cheeks like the white paper filigree over a Valentine . . . (*BG* 1)

They met a friend of her father with his little boy who 'lifted the little
girl's veil, and boldly planted a kiss on her cheek'. In *Literature* this
charming but not apparently significant event in the child's life is
related to Dicky's instinct for words by the fact that he discovers that
the little girl he has kissed has returned to Troy – in fact, on Hudson
– and when he asks his parents about 'this far-off, mysterious and yet
not wholly unknown sound' his father murmurs Marlowe's lines
about Helen of Troy. His father repeats the lines at Dicky's request:

> . . . His father's citation awakened in Dicky's memory the poignant
> cadences of David's lament. The new words had the same mysterious
> power, gave him the same sense of knowing something he couldn't tell;
> and henceforth every word and cluster of words endowed with that
> power grouped themselves about this little nucleus of music, building up
> an enchanted island of sound to which his fancy could put off at will. He
> grew, in after years, to mistrust his infant memories, and to suspect
> himself of unconsciously elaborating them, but he could have sworn that
> when, a year or two later, he chanced on the Island of Epipsychidion,
>   'washed by soft blue Oceans of young air'.
> he knew it at once for his own Isle of Sounds . . . (*LIT*, Dr 2.)

Vance Weston too responds initially to the sounds of words before he
begins to explore them as literature: the Bible's 'haunting words and
cadences were the richest of his mental possessions' (*HRB* 19) and
when he sits down in the library at 'The Willows' for the first time
and reads 'Kubla Khan' he thinks: 'Oh what beautiful, what incredible
words! What did they mean? But what did it matter what they
meant? Or whether they meant anything but their own unutterable
music?' (*HRB* 50).

Further manifestations of Dicky's vocation, incidents that presage
his future, are closely based on those in Edith Wharton's own
childhood: in particular, the urge to read aloud to an audience, to
communicate treasures discovered in literature, and the impulse to
'make-up' stories even before being able to write. Does she distance
herself sufficiently from these experiences and feelings to transmute
them into art? She was aware of the problem of using autobiographical
material for fiction: she discusses the autobiographical tale at the end
of the chapter 'Constructing a Novel' in *The Writing of Fiction* and
distinguishes 'the born novelist' from the 'authors of self-confession
in novel form' by 'the absence of the objective faculty in the latter'.
The born novelist can transform his own experiences into fiction

through 'a brain working objectively': she cites as examples of successful autobiographical novels Tolstoy's *The Kreutzer Sonata* and Goethe's *Werther*.

Her belief that writers are born before they can be made, that innate instinct for language must exist for education to develop and order, is basic to her portrayal of the artist in fiction, in criticism or in autobiography. Why, given this romantic view of the writer as one who possesses an innate gift and a 'sacred impulse' toward creativity, does she leave out the early years of Vance Weston? Without descriptions of his childhood predispositions and experiences which reveal them it is difficult to accept him as a 'born novelist'. Another possible reason for discarding the childhood experience of Dick Thaxter along with the character himself and replacing him with Vance whose story begins at the age of sixteen is that she may have felt that she had not achieved the 'attitude of detachment from [her] subject' that she says in *The Writing of Fiction* distinguishes the creative imagination from the 'merely sympathetic'. And yet, although Vance is a youth at the beginning of the novel he is as much a child intellectually as Dick and is seen to pass through the same stages and reveal the same instinct for language as the earlier writer–hero and Edith Wharton herself. Certainly, even without the childhood and without the evident that *Literature* with its distinctly autobiographical basis existed as an earlier version of the Vance Weston novels, there has been little doubt in the minds of the few critics who mention *Hudson River Bracketed* and *The Gods Arrive* that they are auto-biographical novels. R.W.B. Lewis called the former 'partly disguised or explicit autobiography' (*RWBL* 446) and the latter 'an odd, disguised form of autobiography' (*RWBL* 503). Louis Auchincloss goes as far as to call Vance Weston 'an extension of Mrs Wharton's vision of herself, freed from the impediments of her sex, generation, background, and perhaps more importantly, freed of her own preoccupation with the details of the physical world' (Afterword to *HRB* 1962). Bell (1966), with slightly different emphasis, writes: '*Hudson River Bracketed* and *The Gods Arrive* compose a parable of the modern writer's life which is invaluable to the student of Mrs Wharton's own career and personality' (p. 301). Tuttleton in 'Edith Wharton: Epistemology of Artistic Creation' (1968) discusses at length 'the vexed question of the novel as a form in relation to the confession or autobiography', and points out to some of the similarities between Vance's development and ideas and Mrs Wharton's opinions and beliefs. If she felt that she had not distanced herself from Richard Thaxter, it would appear that neither did she succeed in disguising the autobiographical elements in the Vance Weston novels. The dramatic presentation in the first two chapters of *Literature* compares favourably with the early scenes of *Hudson River Bracketed*, which are unconvincing in portrayal of setting and character and, particularly, in use of dialogue.

The sixty-nine pages of manuscript cover Chapter VI to Chapter IX and one page of the ending to Chapter V: that is, of all of Book II as it stands in the final draft, and the last chapter of Book I. In contrast to the neatness of the scenario and the chapter summaries, the manuscript is reassuringly messy – and, as such, a convincing first draft. While never illegible, her writing is noticeably less neat than it is in the notebook even at the end of these early stages. Possibly this is due to her practice, normal by this time, of writing her novels in bed where she wrote in ink (on one occasion spilt on her host, Howard Sturgis's, sheets) on large sheets of blue letter paper which 'were allowed to drift to the floor thence to be rescued by her secretary and carried away to be typed' (RWBL 4). The manuscript is heavily corrected and many pages are made up of several pieces of paper gummed together revealing a rearrangement of paragraphs (see Appendix VII). Despite her assertion in *A Backward Glance* that 'as soon as the dialogue begins, I become merely a recording instrument, and my hand never hesitates because my mind has not to choose' there is no significant differences between the dialogue and the narrative passages in either the number or type of corrections.

The manuscript appears far from painstakingly written for the writing is sweeping and flowing, often a scrawl. It gives the impression of being the expression of thoughts that come faster than the author's hand can write them down. (The translator into French of *The Age of Innocence*, Mme Saint-René Taillandier, says: 'she wrote rapidly, I believe, after long pondering and maturing of her theme' (PL 155); the appearance of this manuscript seems to confirm this.) She occasionally seems to pass quickly from one alternative to another. For example, on page 89 she moves from 'notice' to 'see' to 'discern'; 'brains' becomes 'intelligence'; 'very handsome' becomes 'very agreeable'; while on page 90, 'while she peered at herself in a tiny mirror' becomes 'reflected in the cracked surface of a gold pocket mirror'. These are slight changes and impossible to evaluate, but overall the alterations tend towards a paring-down and compression.[11] Her 'cut-and-paste' method of ordering means that it is difficult to judge how extensive the re-ordering was but it would appear from the paper, ink and writing, as well as the content, to have been a matter of shifting sentences or paragraphs within a page or two, or rewriting a sentence. For example, the sentences often run over the joins in the paper, which shows that she stuck a fresh piece of paper over a sentence to be rewritten and continued rather than that she chopped up continuous prose and rearranged it. Scissors and paste must have been at her bedside together with the ink.

All alterations to and rearrangement of the manuscript seem to have taken place as she wrote each day or shortly afterwards. She does not make extensive revisions once the manuscript is finished; there are very few minor changes made to the first draft typescript (see Appendix V). It appears that by the time Edith Wharton begins to write she is free to concentrate on composition, on choosing the right word or phrase, because she has planned the novel carefully. The plot, the characters, the setting, the point of view from which the scenes are observed and the distribution of the dramatic scenes within the overall structure of the novel have all been planned, as study of the early stages has shown, leaving the author's imagination free to visualize and realize. By her careful ordering, Edith Wharton gives her fluid imagination a form to fill. Her characters and subject may 'appear' in her mind but it is through systematic method that she turns 'swarming subjects' into art. The apparent paradox of knowing how the story ends but leaving the characters free to arrive there – 'these people of mine, whose ultimate destiny I know so well, walk to it by ways unrevealed to me beforehand' (*BG* 204) – is comprehensible when we see that Edith Wharton, by laying out the plot first, allows herself the freedom to make character the primary concern of her composition. What 'one must call by the old bardic name of inspiration' guides her hand by the manuscript stage of *Literature* in the same way that it had initiated the subject and characters: the technique of fiction has been applied to build up the novel's early stages.

CHAPTER FIVE

The Artist in Society

A Son at the Front (1923) is Edith Wharton's only other novel, besides *Hudson River Bracketed* and *The Gods Arrive*, that has an artist, the painter John Campton, as the central figure. (Ralph Marvell of *The Custom of the Country* is a writer, but only of a gentlemanly dilettante type.) Many of her short stories, particularly the early ones, have as their protagonists authors, painters or connoisseurs, but few are concerned with either aesthetic problems or with the relation between life and art. I have chosen to discuss in conjunction with the Vance Weston novels and *A Son at the Front* the following short stories: 'Souls Belated' from the collection *The Greater Inclination* (1899); 'The Recovery' from *Crucial Instances* (1901); 'The Verdict' from *The Hermit and the Wild Woman* (1908); 'Full Circle' from *Tales of Men and Ghosts* (1910); and 'Writing a War Story' published in *Women's Home Companion* in September 1919. Each of these stories deals with one or more of the issues that confront the artist as a social being and that are also dealt with in greater detail in *Hudson River Bracketed* and *The Gods Arrive*.

There are two interesting if peripheral points to be made about Edith Wharton's fiction about the artist. First, in only two stories, 'The Touchstone' (1900) and 'The Temperate Zone' (1926), are the serious professional artists, both writers, women – and they are dead before the story begins. There are only four other women artists who come even loosely into this category and they are dealt with facetiously. The significance of this may be that Edith Wharton felt that the particular problems of the woman artist might have dominated the problems for artists in general which she wished to emphasize. Secondly, her early novels – before 1923 – are not concerned with the artist, whereas in the early short stories artists predominate among the protagonists. For example, in her two earliest collections of short stories, *The Greater Inclination* (1899) and *Crucial Instances* (1901), nine stories out of fifteen are about artists, whereas in her two last collections (excluding *Ghosts*), *Human Nature* (1933) and *The World Over* (1936), only one, 'A Glimpse', out of a total of twelve, has artists, musicians, as protagonists. ('Joy in the House' has an off-stage painter.) The fact that Edith Wharton wrote fiction about the artist, whether short stories or novels, throughout her life confirms that, as she wrote to W.C. Brownell, the subject was 'dear to her heart'. Her reasons for writing stories and not novels about the artist early in her career may have been, given that she saw 'situation [as] the main concern of the short story, character of the novel', that she was saving the more complex and important material concerning the artist's nature for the long-contemplated central work while exploring different 'situations' in the stories. It would seem that once *Hudson River Bracketed* and *The Gods Arrive*, her central works about the artists, were under way she no longer felt the need to explore the subject in the short story as well.

Edith Wharton's artist is firmly tethered in the real world where money, love, manners, houses, clothes, food, or lack of them, impinge on his inner world as well as being the material from which he creates. All her central characters whether artists or not experience difficulty in reconciling the ideal with the real world: the choices lie between convention or freedom, responsibility or egoism, society or individual will, fashion or taste. The artist with his special sensibility and intensity of personal vision has particular problems in harmonizing the outer and inner worlds and in balancing their sometimes conflicting claims. He cannot escape the demands of society and individuals and he needs to apply to his life as much as his art the principles of order, harmony, continuity, taste and tradition if he is to function as an artist and a social being. The domestic aspect of the real world which, as with the public aspect, both promotes and hinders the artist's activities, is most often explored in Edith Wharton's fiction via the issue of marriage. In this relationship the structures and conventions which govern society's manners and morals and the personal or individual need for human relationship meet. In exploring the artist's attitude to marriage, therefore, Edith Wharton finds an opportunity to examine his relationship with convention and order as well as with his own emotional needs. Indeed, marriage in these stories often presents itself as an issue – a choice, a threat to independence, a relationship with the potential to strengthen or undermine the individual's sense of identity. Marriage also occasionally provides a perspective in the work, as the judgements of a partner are used to complement or contradict the artist–hero's view of himself and his opinions, thus enlarging our view of him and of the issues.

Marriage for the artist – and, indeed, for all her main characters – is shown by Edith Wharton to represent all the advantages and disadvantages of order, reason, tradition and social convention. Against it stand the attractions of freedom, impulse and individuality. In the life of the artist no less than in art Edith Wharton valued spontaneity and freedom of the spirit but, equally, esteemed reason and the structure of standards outside the individual. Her belief in principles based on traditional values was not founded on a sense of the needs of society but wholly on a sense of what the artist needs in order to develop and survive. Convention is a distillation, and sometimes a distortion, of traditional wisdom that the individual ignores at his peril – a poor Lily Bart, who created one work of art,[1] herself, perishes because she flouts convention – and part of social convention is marriage. Edith Wharton shows marriage as desirable for the stability of the individual, even the artist, not as necessary for the stability of society: as Frenside says to Halo in *The Gods Arrive*: 'We most of us need a frame-work, a support – the maddest lovers do. Marriage may be too tight a fit – may dislocate and deform. But it shapes life too; prevents growing lopsided or drifting' (*GA* 317).

That Frenside is yet again expressing the author's view is confirmed by a similar awareness in all her fiction and from one of the few times she 'spoke out' in a moment of intimacy to a close friend, Charles du Bois: 'Ah, the poverty, the miserable poverty, of any love that lies outside of marriage, of any love that is not a living together, a sharing of all!' (PL 100). This is not the outburst of one who has never felt or imagined the attractions of breaking away from conventions, but of one who understood and had weighed up the advantages and disadvantages of marriage and free love. Her heroes and heroines are seen either to sacrifice their impulses and desires to the demands of society – Newland Archer, Charity Royal – or to suffer retribution if they do not – Darrow, Lily Bart, Kate Clephane, Ethan Frome. For the artist, the constraints of society, marriage in particular, nevertheless often appears irksome and a threat to the freedom and individuality which are equally necessary to him.

The arguments for and against marriage for the artist, which become important themes in the Vance Weston novels, are dramatized in the short story 'Souls Belated' published in her first collection of stories in 1899. Edith Wharton uses three themes in this story connected specifically with the artist which she takes up and develops in subsequent stories and novels. First, the writer needs change and variety in his milieu, including his intimates; secondly, he has the ability and need to cut himself off from those around him, even the woman he loves; 'He stood before her with the vivid preoccupied stare of the novelist on the trail of a "subject"' (*GL* 100); thirdly, the lover who begins by being necessary to his inspiration becomes the very reason for his failing to write – 'And after all, he had not written a line since they had been together!' (*GL* 101) – and he longs to break free. None of these needs is easily accommodated within marriage.

In 'Souls Belated' Ralph Gannett, a 'promising' novelist, puts the case for marriage while his mistress, with whom he has run away, argues against it. The story opens with them on a train uneasily avoiding the subject, having just heard that her divorce is through: 'It was one of the misfortunes of their situation that they were never busy enough to necessitate, or even justify, the postponement of unpleasant discussions' (*GL* 84). Lydia Tillotson, the mistress, says toward the end of the story: 'I begin to see what marriage is for. It's to keep people away from each other' (*GL* 121). Vance and Halo, unmarried, at times 'seemed too close to each other, seemed to be pressing on each other, pinning down each other's souls' (*GA* 75). Lydia, from whose point of view the story is told apart from the final short section when Gannett's angle of vision is employed, wants an ideal love free from convention whereas Gannett realistically knows that 'life is made up of compromises'. She shrinks, as Halo Tarrant does, from the thought that her lover might feel he ought to marry her because she has left husband and respectability behind for his sake: she felt 'the fear of unwillingly involving Gannett in the trammels of her dependence' (*GL* 90). Halo tells Frenside: 'Even if he [i.e. Tarrant] was to give me my freedom tomorrow I shouldn't tell Vance . . . because the only thing I care for is *his* freedom. I want him to feel as free air' (*GA* 318). When Lydia argues with Gannet with some logic: 'It may be necessary that the world should be ruled by conventions – but if we believed in them why did we break through them?', he replies pragmatically: 'One may believe in them or not; but as long as they do rule the world it is only by taking advantage of their protection that one can find a *modus vivendi*' (*GI* 97). When Lydia and Halo find themselves exposed without this protection in the world, they feel the icy blast of society's disapproval.

The rest of 'Souls Belated' is devoted to proving Gannett's point. Lydia comes to recognize the expediency of accepting society's rules not because of the disapproval of those who uphold those rules but, paradoxically, because she is recognized as a fellow rebel against convention by a woman with a notorious reputation. Lydia recoils from her fellow rebel in moral indignation but realizes her hypocrisy in doing so and in having pretended to be married: 'Respectability! It was one thing in life that was sure I didn't care about, and it's grown so precious to me that I've stolen it because I couldn't get it any other way' (*GI* 120). At the end of the story, Gannett watches her go towards the ferry to leave him rather than give into convention but sees her turn back towards him and marriage and away from her ideal freedom. Gannett himself has reached the point that Lydia had foreseen: 'Even had his love lessened, he was bound to her now by a hundred ties of pity and self-reproach; and she, poor child! must turn back to him as Latude returned to his cell . . .' (*GI* 128).

Implicit in 'Souls Belated' is the idea that the writer's motives are selfish rather than moral: Gannett cannot work until he has order in his life and until he can move freely and unobtrusively in the world; clearly his work matters more to him than convention, morality or even than Lydia. The compromises he is prepared to make are for the sake of his art not for the sake of his lover or for some abstract morality. This egoism, the egoism of genius, prefigures Vance Weston's. Vance is largely blind at first to the social and emotional complications and disorder that his elopement with Halo, still married to Lewis Tarrant, brings to her. Conversely, she brings into his life domestic order which he has never before experienced – 'Nobody every fixed me up like this before' – and he is unaware, unlike Gannett, of the disorder which society perceives in their illicit union until it is forced on his attention.

Edith Wharton uses the issue of marriage in *Hudson River Bracketed* and *The Gods Arrive* to illuminate her beliefs about the importance of the artist of, on the one hand, order and tradition, and, on the other, of personal freedom, a freedom as much from guilt and inconvenience as to live alone in the inner world of his imagination: the 'chains' of marriage give him 'wings'. The marriage issue in the two novels is dramatized in three ways: Vance's marriage to Laura Lou, his long-term extra-marital relationship with Halo and his liaison with Floss Delaney. Each of these relationships highlights, from different angles, the artist's problems in harmonizing the real world with his creative life. With Laura Lou, Vance moves within the framework of marriage from ideal love through despair to a loving acquiescence: in the last months of her life Vance thinks that 'after all, perhaps she was the kind of wife an artist ought to have' (*GA* 373). This marriage demonstrates Edith Wharton's point that marriage – order – however galling at times, is the only solution to love, because it prevents an easy escape from difficulties. She shows that Vance's idealization of Laura Lou, characterized by the romantic metaphors he uses for her – 'my dove', 'a cool moonlit pool', 'a tropical shell with the sun shining through it', 'her lashes were planted like the double row of microscopic hummingbird feathers in a South American embroidery' – quickly becomes reality; she becomes simply 'a human being to be fed, clothed and cherished'. She is his Dora Copperfield, and Vance, like David, learns to accept his wife's limitations, to accept reality and even profit from it. Like Dora, Laura Lou is an incompetent housekeeper, an inadequate companion, 'she seems fated never to keep step with him', a hopeless helper, but Vance feels himself, despite the difficulties and irritations – or because of them – inexorably bound to her and when he is offered a way out of the marriage by her mother he realizes that 'a million delicate tendrils, of which he was unconscious when he and she were together, tightened about his heart and held it fast to hers, in a strange bondage closer than that of love or desire' (*HRB* 276). With Halo, once the illusion of 'predestined happiness' fades when 'the deeper workings of his imagination were no longer aroused by her presence' (*GA* 111), Vance's liberty means that he uses it as licence 'to wound, and escape the consequences' and they drift apart. Even when he returns to her at the end it is reluctantly and almost accidentally. The fact that Vance contemplates marriage with Floss about whom he has no illusions seems to indicate that the lesson he has learned is that marriage must be based on reality not on a vision of the ideal; the fact that he is ultimately appalled by her blackmailing business deal shows that even at this late stage he has still to learn that reality lies with the familiar and everyday, in the world and not in the imagination, in Halo as she really is, not in a 'goddess'. The artist with his unique powers of imagination inevitably finds it harder to accept the pedestrian limitations of marriage – 'most artists are incurably polygamous' – than normal mortals, but must learn to do so because he needs reality without losing sight of the ideal.

In the same way Edith Wharton recognizes and asserts the stabilizing effects of marriage (incorporating domestic routine and social acceptance) she sees, too, that the artist is more likely to benefit from the possession of money than not. Although she satirizes those who replace moral values with material values – Undine Spragge, Floss Delaney, Mrs Glaisher, the new rich societies in *The House of Mirth* and *The Children* – she never shows lack of money as ennobling: money is a necessity. Poverty in Edith Wharton's novels appears rather as debasing and destructive: Lily Bart perishes; escape for Charity Royall and Ethan Frome is impossible; the Bunner sisters are ground down. For the artist, money and worldly success in themselves present no barrier to true aesthetic values: his problem is not that money is a corrupting influence but that lack of money is a distraction. Vance's financial worries take his mind off his work, although lack of them does not liberate his genius as much as he expects; Vyse, Betton's secretary in 'Full Circle', finds his talent

corroded by poverty; John Campton regrets his inability to provide
for his son and finds it distracting. Money is as necessary to the
preservation and encouragement of great art as it is to the individual
artist: Vance thinks of the rich as a 'priestly caste' whose task should
be to have and preserve objects of beauty. Jack Gisburn may not be a
great artist but 'his wife's big bank balance enabled him, with an
appearance of perfect good-breeding, to transmute it into objects of
art and luxury' (*HWW* 198). Edith Wharton's essentially practical
and rational approach to money, as seen in her travel books and her
letters and diaries, is no less obvious in her fiction about the artist.

Halo's journey from idealism to reality follows a similar path,
although a longer and more difficult one, to that of Lydia Tillotson
over thirty years earlier. Her perspective on marriage and on Vance's
views further illuminates the issues, as seen by Edith Wharton, of
freedom versus convention and of traditional structures and values
challenged by the will of the individual. Halo begins by rejoicing in
their freedom from conventional bonds: 'In heaven there's no
marrying or giving in marriage. Let's stay in heaven as long as we can'
(*GA* 61) which echo Lydia's words at the beginning of 'Souls
Belated': 'No ceremony is needed to consecrate our love for each
other.' Halo is soon brought up against the social realities and forced
to face firstly, her ambivalence towards marriage – she is proud of
their breaking free from convention but hates not being married
when she is denied a social position – and secondly, the difference
between her attitude, stemming from her social and family background, and Vance's: 'There were moments when Vance's moral
simplicity was more trying than the conventionalities she had fled
from' (*GA* 53). Edith Wharton in this situation uses her young
Barbarian from the West on the one hand to point out the hypocrisies
of conventional traditional attitudes and, on the other, to satirize the
black and white attitudes of the New World. Convention puts
appearances above the needs of the individual whereas the modern
man puts the desires and even comfort of the individual before social
order. Halo's point of view – 'he had unwittingly offended the very
prejudices from which she imagined he had delivered her' (*GA* 58) –
underlines for the reader the opposition between their attitudes
which reflects the gulf between the societies from which they come.

Edith Wharton shows the confusion in Halo and Vance's views
about marriage as stemming not only from their individual characters
but also from their backgrounds. She satirizes and contrasts the social
codes of New York and the Midwest which, disparate in their
principles, are united in valuing the marriage ceremony. Halo
confronts the incompatibility of her behaviour with the code in
which she had been brought up, between her conscious breaking free

and her ingrained knowledge that restraint is necessary. She sees during their argument in Spain that the society in which she had grown up 'had been regulated by a code of which Vance did not know the first word, and she saw how such tacit observances may be interwoven with the closest human intimacies' (*GA* 59). Halo has felt that their passion was strong enough to ignore convention so that when she finds she cares about being a social outcast she doubts the strength of their love. She resolves to prove that her passion is greater than her inherited prejudices and that she cares more for Vance's freedom than her position: she assures him that she does not mind if she never has her divorce and is able to marry him. The honesty of Halo's thoughts – even if she evades their logical outcome – is contrasted with the hypocrisy of the family and society whose values she cannot help sharing. Her mother, Mrs Spear, who coquettes with Bohemianism, had married out of her own class but 'it was a defiance sanctioned by church and law, and she had never dreamed of her daughter's taking liberties with those institutions.' She felt that 'she was a Lorburn of Paul's Landing, and people of pre-revolutionary stock, however emancipated their sympathies, conformed to tradition in their conduct' (*GA* 32). The values of Vance's family from the Midwest, inimical to those of Old New York, nevertheless impose on him a certain embarrassment about their elopement: 'Of course I know how my mother feels about marriage in general . . . The marriage ceremony is a kind of fetish to her' (*GA* 55). But the reason for this reverence was not based on tradition but was rather part of the New America's worship of the new – so frequently satirized by Edith Wharton in *Hudson River Bracketed* – which did not preclude a snobbish appreciation as well as contempt of 'Old' Society:

> He understood that his life with Halo was something to be accounted for and explained away, and that the pride the family had felt in his prospective marriage ('a Park Avenue affair', as Mrs Weston had boasted) increased the mortification of having to own that it had not taken place. 'Some fuss about a divorce – don't they *have* divorce in the Eastern states, anyhow?' she enquired sardonically, as if no lack of initiative would surprise her in the original Thirteen. (*GA* 362)

The difference between the social code of Old New York and that of the Midwest, as embodied in the Spears and the Westons, is that the conventions by which the former live have a basis of traditional wisdom whereas for the latter they are based on expediency and ignorance. For Vance, once he adopts the wider perspective and taste of an older society, it is easy to discard the superficial values of his upbringing, and with them the conventions, however deep-rooted, of any society: but for Halo the desire for a love free from conventional restraints conflicts with her continued respect for the traditional forms in which she was brought up.

When Halo gets to Paris the attitudes of the Bohemian crowd around her brother, Lorry, make her realize how much traditional standards mean to her, with their basis of order and reason:

> Free love, she found, was not the simple experiment she had imagined. The coast of Bohemia might be pleasant to land on for a picnic, yet the interior of the country proved disappointing. She had fancied that in the tolerant air of her brother's studio she would shake off this feeling. She knew it was not based on moral scruples (morally speaking the business was still a labyrinth to her) but on a sort of inherited dislike of being unclassified, and out of the social picture. . . . But from the first she had felt herself an outsider in this world which was to set her free . . . she had dropped out of the picture without yet fitting into this one. . . . Beauty, order and reasonableness grew more and more dear to her in the noisy anarchy of Lorry's circle. (GA 84–5)

Like Lydia, who is pulled up short by the attitude of the vulgar Mrs Copt in the same position as herself, Halo is jarred into facing reality by offence against taste rather than morals. For all the value Edith Wharton places on 'moral vision' in a novelist, it seems that in her central characters moral sensibility is replaced by taste, defined in *French Ways and their Meaning* as 'the recognition of a standard'. Certainly, she puts no moral case for marriage: Halo's position as Vance's mistress is offensive because she has, through education and instinct, aesthetic judgement and therefore is incapable of accepting the shoddy in any sphere. Her brother Lorry points out to her that 'when a lady's such a lady, all the night-life and the adultery won't wipe out the damned spot . . . I'm sorry; but you offend me aesthetically' (GA 92). As if to underline the point, Halo is cut dead as she leaves Lorry's studio by vulgar Mrs Glaisher whose 'every act and attitude' was 'the outcome of a prolonged and conscientious study of what her particular world approved and disapproved of' (GA 96). Vance, as a result of *his* meeting with Mrs Glaisher, is forced to think of Halo's position. The night before he had thought of marriage.

> How did two people who had once filled each other's universe manage to hold together as the tide receded? Why, by the world-old compulsion of marriage, he supposed. Marriage was a trick, a sham, if you looked at it one way; but it was the only means man had yet devised for defending himself against his own frivolity. He was struck by something august and mysterious in the fact of poor humanity's building up this barrier against

itself. To the Catholic church marriage was a divine institution; but it seemed to him infinitely more impressive as an emanation of the will of man. (*GA* 120)

And after his dinner with Mrs Glaisher, who makes her attitude toward Halo clear to him, his eyes are opened toward Halo's position:

> She had sacrificed with a light heart her standing among her own kind; but something deeper than her prejudices or her convictions, something she could sacrifice to no one because it was closer to her than reason or passion, made it impossible for her to feel at ease in the new life she had chosen. (*GA* 139)

These thought drive him to a disastrous interview with Lewis Tarrant to ask him to divorce or be divorced and leave Halo free to marry her lover. Tarrant and his attitude to marriage demonstrate the detrimental effects of convention by which he has become imprisoned: 'when a man had disciplined himself out of all impulsiveness he stood powerless on the brink of deeper feelings' (*GA* 148). He represents all that is narrow and limiting in conventional attitudes; Vance represents impulse without the knowledge and discipline that a traditional background gives. Tarrant knows the 'accepted formulas' but cannot cope with 'the agony of envy, jealousy and resentment battling together in his soul'; Vance understands his own and Tarrant's feelings and instincts but 'was ignorant of the language in which men of Tarrant's world have been schooled to disguise their thoughts' (*GA* 150). In these two characters, Edith Wharton's clear-sighted view of the damage and the benefits that social forms can impart is incarnate.

Edith Wharton shows the differences between the artist's particular problems in dealing with personal relationships and with society and those of the ordinary mortal by alternating the point of view between Vance and Halo in both *Hudson River Bracketed* and *The Gods Arrive*.[2] Vance is the centre of Halo's world and even her growing need for marriage is less important than his special needs: nothing mattered 'except that she should go on serving and inspiring this child of genius with whom a whim of the gods had entrusted her' (*GA* 105). Edith Wharton contrasts this unselfishness with the selfishness of the artist by then showing us Vance's thoughts: his inner world is of paramount importance and any threat to it must be overcome:

> She seemed to resent whatever excluded her from his pursuits; but though it troubled him to hurt her he could not give up the right to live his inner life in his own way, and the conflict disquieted and irritated him. (*GA* 111)

But however selfish the artist may feel justified in being, outside his periods of creative fervour – 'during those week of mysterious brooding he had not once thought of what Halo would think or say' – he cannot ignore other individuals or society. By placing Halo as the centre of consciousness in over a third of *The Gods Arrive* Edith Wharton shows the suffering caused by the artist's need to escape domestic and social ties. Left alone she realizes that she thinks of her life only in relation to her love for Vance and speculates on the reason for his detachment from her. Her jealousy of his intellectual companions becomes ordinary sexual jealousy and wild conjectures as to whom he is with. The switch to Vance's point of view shows both how little the ordinary mortal understands the creative mind – he is, in fact, alone and absorbed by ideas for his new book and problems of technique – and also, conversely, that Halo is right and the artist is simply a man like any other, for Vance's later infidelity is prefigured by his romantic yearnings for the 'magic of the unknown' awakened by the sight of a girl asleep in the wood. His thoughts the next day about his treatment of Halo – he 'wondered how he, who vibrated to every pang of the being he created, could have been so unperceiving and unfeeling' (GA 120) – signify his return to reality from his visionary state. In this real world he feel she needs marriage to protect himself from the 'licence to wound'.

The effect of alternating the point of view of the ordinary individual, Halo, with that of the artist is to give the reader a balanced and wider understanding of, amongst other issues, marriage. Our knowledge of the thought processes of both protagonists means that their conversations on the subject are ironically undercut by our judgement of what they say. This judgement represents a third point of view which is objective in that it stands outside the novel. For example, in the conversation between Halo and Vance on his return to Paris which ends Book II and their Paris period, we know that, while Vance tells Halo she is free to do as she likes, she is longing for him to reaffirm his love and commitment and that, despite his declaration that he hates not being married, all his instincts are crying out for the freedom to form new relationships and create new works of art. We understand the needs of both and that marriage could provide the stability that Halo needs and the boundaries which would leave Vance free to explore and expand within them.

Unlike the protagonists of 'Souls Belated' who are free to marry when it becomes obvious to them that it is what they both need, Halo and Vance are unable to use that convenient structure provided by society to protect individuals from themselves and the outside world. Despite a time of peace together in the South of France when Vance looking at Halo 'felt in his breast a new emotion . . . as if out of their loving and quarrelling, the uneasy blazing and smouldering of their passion, something winged and immortal had sprung, and brooded over them' (GA 194), their relationship is slowly eroded by Vance's need to escape and his affair with Floss Delaney, by Halo's refusal to assert herself out of respect for Vance's freedom and genius, and by her lack of frankness with herself, Vance or her old friend Frenside. Frenside comes to see Halo, who is alone in France, as adviser and ambassador from Lewis Tarrant who is now willing to give her a divorce. Halo declares that she will not tell Vance because he would feel obliged to marry her – as Lydia Tillotson feels she has put her lover in the position that he was bound to 'stand the damage'. Frenside makes the essential point – and speaks for Edith Wharton and the voice of common sense – that there is nothing so binding as an invisible bond on the one hand and that, on the other, true freedom can only be attained through accepting boundaries:

> The untrammelled artist. Well, I don't believe it's the ideal state for the artist, any more than it is for the retail grocer. We all of us seem to need chains – and wings . . . How do you know you're not chaining him up all the tighter? The defenceless woman, and all that. If you were his wife, you and he'd be on the same level. (GA 318–9)

He also makes the point that Vance in his approach to Tarrant has shown that he cares about marriage. Halo says that he forgot about it 'when I pretended I didn't care . . . What's loving but pretending?' The irony is that only a truly honest woman could be so dishonest. Meanwhile, as the reader knows, Vance has been 'drowned in the wild current' of love for Floss. Her old friend's visit makes Halo realize that 'she had wanted the absolute – and life had handed her one of its usual shabby compromises, and she had not known what to do with it' (GA 322). By this time when she at last comes to the realization that everyone, even the artist and the maddest lover – 'perhaps the maddest most of all' – needs the double protection of marriage, protection from other people and protection from the inevitable fluctuations of feeling, she and Vance are too far apart. Vance's grandmother, the voice of natural as opposed to sophisticated wisdom in the novels, tells him:

> It's the daily wear and tear, and the knowing- it's-got-to-be-made-to-do, keeps people together; not making eyes at each other by moonlight . . . I'd say it's the worries that make married folks sacred to each other – and what do you two know of all that?' (GA 374)

This makes Vance think back to his marriage to Laura Lou where the irritating friction of familiarity had made separation unthinkable, while in regard to himself and Halo, their perpetual mutual insistence on not being a burden to each other, on scrupulously respecting each other's freedom, had somehow worn the tie thin instead of strengthening it. (*GA* 375)

Edith Wharton's exploration of the benefits and disadvantages of marriage for the artist demonstrates her belief in the necessity for order in private and public lives which requires compromise of the ideal with the actual. She often uses the word 'compromise' in connection with marriage as she uses images of imprisonment: Lydia and Gannett make a compromise with convention in accepting the 'bondage' of marriage on their free love; Lydia turns back as to a 'cell' from freedom; Vance and Halo compromise in accepting that their love has not survived without the framework of marriage and are prepared, nevertheless, to enter a life together – and presumably marriage – knowing that their love is no longer ideal and 'untrammelled'. Both couples put on the 'bonds' of matrimony without which their relationship falls apart and bow to the accepted standards of society. The recognition and acceptance of standards, proportion and rules, recurrent values in all Edith Wharton's work, are for the artist as mandatory in his life as in his art.

Edith Wharton's treatment of the issue of marriage shows the tyranny of social censorship at the same time as it endorses marriage as an 'order' or a 'form; within which the individual who corrects excessive idealism can find relationship or autonomy. This superficial social censorship, based rather on appearances than morality, has its aesthetic counterpart in the tyrannies of fashion and provinciality in the world of art. This favourite butt of Edith Wharton's criticisms becomes the occasion in a number of her fictions for the exploration of the artist in relation to public social life. From the stories and novels concerned with the artist's relationship with his public and different social groups it can be clearly seen that Edith Wharton believed that the artist must learn and maintain taste and judgement in conditions where fashion and false values are often seductive. A particular danger for the successful artist lies in the flattery of his admirers which may lead him to accept his art at the valuation of those of superficial vision rather than to measure himself against the absolute standards of the great masters. In making these points, Edith Wharton has the opportunity to dramatize some of her familiar grievances against critics and the public, against the poverty of American values and against those who wish to destroy the past in order to create a new form of art. She often dramatizes these views by employing the consciousness of an unsophisticated but intelligent character to reflect the action while at the same time giving her own point of view through the use of irony.

* * *

'The Recovery' (1901) is a story which asserts the importance to the artist of striving towards an absolute standard of quality in his art which can only be recognized by measuring himself against the standards of the past. The corresponding need to acquire taste and judgement beyond a provincial background and the dictates of fashion is also crucial. Edith Wharton dramatizes these ideas by showing the painter, Keniston's, discovery of great art and his relationship with an undiscerning public. Keniston, a native of Hillbridge, U.S.A., where he is much admired, discovers the great masters when he takes an exhibition of his work to Paris and discovers that measured against these standards his art is non-existent. He is artist enough to recognize this and courageous enough to resolve to begin again to learn to paint. Edith Wharton employs the consciousness of an intelligent woman close to the artist – as she does in the Vance Weston novels – to discover the artist's deficiencies and development and, through her own change from provincial to woman of taste, to add counterpoint. Claudia Day at the beginning of the story is an ignorant and impressionable young woman on her first visit to Hillbridge, the seat of the powerful genius, Keniston:

> In East Onondaigua, where she lived, Hillbridge was looked on as an Oxford. Magazine writers, with the easy American use of the superlative, designated it as 'the venerable *alma mater*', 'the antique seat of learning', and Claudia Day had been brought up to regard it as the fountain-head of knowledge, and of that mental distinction which is so much rarer than knowledge. (*CI 88–9*)

The prevailing tone of the early part of the story set in Hillbridge is ironic and betrays the authorial presence behind the fictional point of view satirizing the poverty of American culture with its ignorance of the wealth of the past contained in the European tradition. Measured by any other standard than that of their provincial setting Keniston's paintings disappear:

> To 'know' Keniston one must come to Hillbridge. Never was work more dependent for its effect on 'atmosphere', on *milieu*. Hillbridge was Keniston's *milieu*, and there was one lady, a devotee of his art, who went so far as to assert that once, at an exhibition in New York, she had passed a Keniston without recognizing it. (*CI 86*)

Keniston himself, as long as he remains in Hillsbridge, accepts the admiration of his public as his due.

In the second section of the story, Claudia has been married to the painter for ten years and now looks sceptically at Mrs Davenant, one of her husband's most fervent admirers: 'young, credulous, and emotionally extravagant: she reminded Claudia of her earlier self'. Claudia, during her decade of marriage, has developed a sense of an absolute standard: 'That innate sense of relativity, which even East Onondaigua had not been able to check in Claudia Day, had been fostered in Mrs Keniston by the artistic absolutism of Hillbridge' (*CI* 94). She is further made uneasy by her husband's comfortable satisfaction in his work. Claudia's original vision of Keniston as an ideal Artist is eroded by her experience of his attitude, which she knows instinctively is not that of the true artist:

> What perplexed her was Keniston's satisfaction in his achievement. She had always imagined that the true artist must regard himself as the imperfect vehicle of the cosmic emotion – that beneath every difficulty overcome a new one lurked, the vision widening as the scope enlarged. (*CI* 95)

Claudia, like Halo, had had 'her vision of an intellectual communion which should admit her to the inmost precincts of his inspiration' (*CI* 96). But the artist does not want intellectual companionship from his women: Vance even thinks that 'intellectual comradeship was unattainable; that was not the service women could render men' (*GA* 390). Claudia, excluded from her husband's thoughts, becomes critical: 'if he worked slowly, it was not because he mistrusted his powers of expression, but because he had really so little to express' (*CI* 96).

Although critical of her husband's nature, Claudia's confidence in his art remains as long as they stay in Hillbridge: 'she was what she always dreamed of being – the wife of a great artist' (CI 99). But once they arrived in Europe that confidence dwindles, while her opinion of his character increases: 'he surprised her by an acuteness of observation that she had sometimes inwardly accused him of lacking' (*CI* 103). In London at the beginning of their journey of aesthetic discovery, a journey that is the precursor of Vance's, she flinches from

> the comparison of her husband's work with what they were daily seeing. Art, she inwardly argued, was too various, too complex, dependent on too many interrelations of feeling and environment, to allow of its being judged by any provisional standard. (*CI* 105)

The concept of absolute standards for art outside any individual artist or environment is grasped by Claudia and Keniston once they move away from their provincial background. Claudia, whose revelation about the nature of art and the inferior quality of her husband's paintings has been shown to the reader, receives the first hint that Keniston's view of his work is undergoing a reassessment similar to her own when he says to his patron from Hillbridge who has accompanied the paintings to Paris:

> 'If my pictures are good enough for anything they oughtn't to need explaining.' Mrs. Davenant stared. 'But I thought that was what made them so interesting!' 'Perhaps it was,' he murmured. (*CI* 110)

A clear statement of Edith Wharton's view of the value of tradition and continuity, harmony and order, and that in France those qualities reign supreme is given through Claudia's consciousness:

> Never had she felt more isolated amid that ordered beauty which gives a social quality to the very stones and mortar of Paris. All about her were evidences of an artistic sensibility pervading every form of life like the nervous structure of the huge frame – a sensibility so delicate, alert, and universal, that it seemed to leave no room for obtuseness or error. (*CI* 111)

She feels isolated because to her 'the significance of the whole vast revelation was centred in the light shed on one tiny spot of consciousness – the value of her husband's work' (*CI* 113). In fact, she is not so much concerned with the value of Keniston's paintings measured against an absolute standard, as with whether he will realize how worthless they are and what he will do if he does realize. When, at last, she steels herself to visit the exhibition, she immediately comprehends that the work has disappeared below the lowest standard of measurement:

> The pictures struck her instantly as odd gaps in the general harmony; it was self-evident that they had not co-operated. They had not been pushing, aggressive, discordant: they had merely effaced themselves. The canvases were all there – and the frames, but the miracle, the mirage of life and meaning, had vanished like some atmospheric illusion. What was it that had happened? And had it happened to *her* or to the pictures . . . argument was swept off its feet by the huge rush of a single conviction – the conviction that the pictures were bad . . . The great vision of beauty through which she had been moving, as one enchanted, was turned to a phantasmagoria of evil-mocking shapes. She hated the past; she hated its splendour, its power, its wicked magical vitality . . . (*CI* 115)

In her hatred of all that belittles her husband as an artist she attempts to belittle her judgement but 'it seemed as though it were a standard outside of herself' (*CI* 116). After she meets her husband at his exhibition in an attitude of despair she begins to feel pity for him: 'Her one hope had been that Keniston should be clear-eyed enough to face the truth . . . But as his image rose before her she felt a sudden half-maternal longing to thrust herself between him and disaster' (*CI* 117). In the event, Keniston triumphs in his self-knowledge and in his resolution for the future:

> 'It takes time,' he continued musingly, 'to get at them to make out what they're saying – the big fellows, I mean. They're not a communicative lot. At first I couldn't make much out of their lingo – it was too different from mine! . . . But I was bound I wouldn't be beaten, and now, today' – he paused a moment to light a match – 'when I went to look at those things of mine it all came over me in a flash. By Jove! It was as if I'd make them all into a big bonfire to light me on my road! . . .
> 'Is there nothing left,' she faltered.
> 'Nothing left? There's everything!' he exulted. 'Why, here I am, not much over forty, and I've found out already!' (*CI* 119)

Keniston demonstrates that he is a true artist by recognizing an absolute standard and that his work does not measure up to that standard, and by his eagerness to learn and see his way forward toward a new vision. Edith Wharton shows in this story, as she does in *Hudson River Bracketed*, that the danger of provincialism is that it circumscribes and limits judgement through complacency or lack of opportunity. She sums up her view in the story 'The Pretext' (1908) where in Wentworth the 'tone' is unmistakable:

> It permeates every part of the social economy, from the *coiffure* of the ladies to the preparation of the food. It has its sumptuary laws as well as its curriculum of learning. It sits in judgement not only on its own townsmen but on the rest of the world – enlightening, criticizing, ostracizing a heedless universe – and non-conformity to Wentworth standards involves obliteration from Wentworth's consciousness. (*HWW* 137)

For the artist to stay within this enclosed world, Euphoria, Old New York, Hillbridge, Wentworth, would be to stifle his art for lack of freedom, stimulation, experience, and knowledge of the art of the past. The hero of 'The Verdict' (1908), the painter Jack Gisburn, has only to take a short step outside his restricted *milieu* to receive a shock from coming face to face with a standard against which his own work appears worthless. He tells the narrator of the story in retrospect why he gave up painting when confronted by the work of a master who, although a contemporary, had founded his art on 'everlasting foundations'. Gisburn is called in to paint a dead painter by his silly widow who wants to have him painted by a fashionable figure. As he begins to paint the artist lying before him, he becomes conscious of the gulf between his painting and that of the master:

> I dashed at the canvas furiously, and tried some of my bravura tricks! But they failed me, they crumbled . . . And how he saw through my lies!
> I looked up again, and caught sight of that sketch of the donkey hanging on the wall near his bed. His wife told me afterward it was the last thing he had done – just a note taken with a shaking hand . . . just a note! But it tells his whole history. There are years of patient scornful persistence in every line. A man who had swum with the current could never have learned that mighty up-stream stroke . . . (*HWW* 189)

The realization of his inferiority brings a double revelation to Gisburn: 'If I could have painted that face . . . I should have done a great thing. The next greatest thing was to see that I couldn't – and that grace was given me.' Unlike Keniston, he feels that it is too late to relearn: 'Begin again? . . . When the one thing that brings me anywhere near him is that I knew enough to leave off? (*HWW* 192). Gisburn, like Keniston and Vance, proves himself to have taste once he moves out of his small circle and has the opportunity to see great art founded on the principles of the past.

The recognition of quality depends on developing taste formed through experiencing the best in art and, to a lesser extent, a wide variety of informed opinion. An artist must beware of accepting the standards of fashion rather than taste – or of his admirers rather than of the past. Admiration can distort the writer's values: Jack Gisburn 'all his life, had been surrounded by interesting women: they had fostered his art, it had been reared in the hot-house of their adulation' (*HWW* 179): Keniston was surrounded by adoring fans at home in Hillbridge. Geoffrey Betton, the hero of 'Full Circle', allows his fan-mail to influence his evaluation of his writing, and his vanity overcomes his judgement: 'But if the professor understood his book, the girl from Florida understood *him*: and Betton was fully alive to the superior qualities of discernment which this implied' (*CSS* 88). The irony of the situation, which is the subject of the story, is that the letters which create a false idea of the value of his work are fakes and have been written by Betton's secretary, an unsuccessful novelist. The skill betrayed by the secretary reveals that he is a better writer than the erstwhile fashionable novelist, Betton, whose own fan letters to himself had been easily spotted by the secretary. Betton admits admiration for the dissembler:

> And so you applied your superior – your immeasurably superior – abilities to carrying on the humbug, and deceiving me as I'd tried to

deceive you. And you did it so successfully that I don't see why the devil you haven't make your fortune writing novels! The way you differentiated your people – characterized them – avoided my stupid mistake of making the women's letters too short and too logical . . . the amount of ingenuity and art you wasted on it! (*CSS* 91)

The foolish fan with an eye to the dictates of fashion rather than taste may inflate an artist's opinion of himself and distort his judgement.

In 'Writing a War Story' (1919) – rightly dismissed by R.W.B. Lewis as a 'flimsy tale' – Edith Wharton satirizes undiscerning criticism and false literary notions by portraying an aspiring young female writer. Ivy Spang, authoress of a little volume of verse called *Vibrations*, is asked to contribute a 'tragedy with a happy ending' to a magazine intended to bring joy to the British war wounded. Her portrait in nurse's uniform will accompany the story to give it added poignancy, for Ivy is very pretty. She retires to the country to devote her mornings – 'for Ivy knew that the morning hours of great authors were always 'sacred' – to writing her story. But she finds the creative process harder than she had imagined: 'why did stories ever begin, and why did they leave off? Life didn't – it just went on and on' (*CSS* 361). She goes for a walk but dare not join her friends 'lest they should frighten away her Inspiration. She knew that Inspirations were fussy and contrarious, and she felt rather as if she were dragging along a reluctant dog on a string' (*CSS* 36). The poor bemused authoress 'decided that, perhaps, if you pretended hard enough that you knew what your story was about, you might end by finding out towards the last page' (*CSS* 362). In desperation Ivy turns to her old governess whose suggestions she treats with scorn: Mademoiselle suggests timidly: 'Suppose you were to begin by thinking of a subject?'

' "Oh, my dear, the subject's nothing!" exclaimed Ivy.' But Mademoiselle persists: 'Still – in writing a story, one has to have a subject. Of course I know it's only the treatment that really matters' (*CSS* 363). Ivy condescends to accept 'one of these artless tales' from Mademoiselle and 'transform it into Literature'. Ivy sits down to 'do battle with the art of fiction' spurred on by the vision of herself in her photograph. The tale once completed and published falls on an uninterested public – but her photograph is a hit. The wounded soldiers ask her for copies of it, but none has read her story. The final humiliation comes when she finds a well-known novelist in the ward laughing over her story. When she asks him to explain why he finds it funny, her answers:

'You've got hold of a wonderfully good subject; and that's the main thing, of course – Ivy interrupted him eagerly. 'The subject's the main thing?'

'Why naturally; it's only the people without invention who tell you it isn't.'

'Oh,' she gasped, trying to readjust her carefully acquired theory of aesthetics.

'You've got hold of an awfully good subject,' Harbard continued: 'but you've rather mauled it, haven't you?' (*CSS* 369)

He adds insult to injury by then asking for a copy of the photograph.

Ivy Spang embodies the false values and false conceptions about the art of fiction that threaten the novelist from his public: even more importantly she embodies the threat to taste and judgement of reducing art to treatment and of trivializing it through replacing traditional standards with those of fashion. In 'Writing a War Story', *Hudson River Bracketed* and *The Gods Arrive* Edith Wharton shows she considers that taste and vision in art can be corrupted by fashion and cliquish prejudice. The substitution of a faulty personal vision, material values of superficial display for order and taste in art and manners and morals as well – as in the New York novels – is often the act of those who, through defective background, breeding or instinct, lack knowledge of sensibility.

Vance Weston experiences a variety of inward-looking and self-satisfied groups. These groups are presented both through Vance's at first naive and then discerning eyes and from an ironic authorial viewpoint. The Spear household is initially presented as slightly absurd: the Spears had intended to be 'a nucleus of intellectual revolt; but the world had revolted without waiting for them. Their heresies were too mild to cause any excitement outside of their own circle' (*HRB* 62). Mrs Spear snatches at the new – she is one of the 'Seekers' who welcomes Vance's grandmother at the end of the novel – but without relinquishing the old. To Vance the Spears 'belonged to a class, a society, a type of people, who naturally breathed this larger air, possessed this privilege of moving freely backward and forward in time and space' (*HRB* 95). Despite a concern with fashionable movement, Halo's family has given her a wide range of reference and knowledge of the past which 'saved her from the passing extravagances of fashion' (*HRB* 137). She and Frenside, that representative of true standards, despise what they term 'germ-carriers', 'people who get every new literary and artistic disease and hand it on' (*HRB* 209).

In spite of her own taste, the group Halo Tarrant gathers around herself in New York is seen by Vance to have but a superficial vision of art. At first he is dazzled to be the centre of the attention of this smart and successful literary set who ask: 'How does it feel to be It?' after the success of his story 'Unclaimed'. He soon discovers, however, that these 'easy affable people' are not concerned with his art or the art of fiction but with trivial questions:

> They wanted to know what else he had written, what he was doing now, when he was going to start in on a novel, when he would have enough short stories for a volume, whether he had thought up any new subjects lately, whether he found it easier to write in a big city or in his own quiet surroundings at home, whether Nature inspired him or he had to be with people to get a stimulus, what his best working hours were, whether he could force himself to write so many hours a day, whether he didn't think a real artist must always be a law unto himself (this from one or two of the younger women), and whether he found he could dictate, or had to type out his own things . . . (*HRB* 213)

Vance is excited by this interest but quickly realizes that his questioners are not interested in the answers. Later among the same group and surrounded by admiration and apparent interest: 'Vance felt how random praise can isolate and discourage. All that made his work worthwhile, all that made the force of his vocation, was apparently invisible or incomprehensible to others' (*HRB* 305).

This trivialization of his art is rejected by Vance while he enjoys the adulation. Frenside warns him that 'nothing is as disintegrating as success' and advises him to follow his own impulse rather than the advice of the critics and his admirers – but at the same time to see as many people as he can: 'Manners are your true material, after all' (*HRB* 287).

Vance spends more time than at the Tarrants' among the would-be Bohemian group that surrounds a sculptress, Rebecca Stram, and meetings in 'The Cocoanut Tree'. Vance thinks

> how wonderful life would be, spent among these fellows who talked of art as if it *were* real estate – a very American Bohemia – circling around literary competitions and rewards. These young people 'want to wipe out the past and get a fresh eye on things. (*HRB* 199)

And, although Vance feels more at ease with this group, he contrasts it unfavourably with the Tarrants',

> where everybody talked and nobody listened, or said anything particularly worth hearing, if you thought it over – but where the look of the rooms and the people had something harmonious and long-related, suggesting a mysterious intelligence between persons and things, an atmosphere as heavy with the Past as that of the library at the Willows. (*HRB* 215)

Vance becomes 'more and more conscious of some deep-seated difference that cut him off from the circumambient literary "brightness", or rather left him unsatisfied by it' (*HRB* 245) and he eventually finds 'he had gone the round of their [i.e. the Stram set] wisdom, and come back still hungry' (*HRB* 328).

Vance takes the measure of the group of artists he meets in Paris –
amongst them Lorry Spear who had wanted back at Eaglewood, on
the Hudson, to teach Halo 'not to have taste' – which also rejected
the past but which contained other worthwhile elements. Vance
recognizes that:

> Their superior cultivation made it impossible to brush aside their theories
> and pronouncements as he had the outpourings of the young men in
> Rebecca Stram's studio; he felt compelled to listen and examine their
> arguments, fallacious as some of them seemed. (*GA* 115)

Those arguments, which at least address seriously the problems for
the writer of fiction, are discarded by Vance for reasons and in a tone
familiar from Edith Wharton's criticism. Vance rejects the notion that
the novel of manners is out of date and that the 'exploration of the
subliminal' is the way forward for the novel: 'The fishers in the turbid
stream-of-consciousness had reduced their fictitious characters to a
bundle of loosely tied instincts and habits, borne along blindly on the
current of existence' (*GA* 116).

But although he does not agree with the new theories, he is
influenced enough to feel dissatisfied with his recent work, *The
Puritan in Spain*, which by its very success with the public proved he
had not done anything more than write a variation on his previous
popular novel. His current work *Colossus* would, he vows, be
different: the very name 'symbolized the new vision, the great firm
outline, that he wanted to project against the petty chaos of Jane
Megg's world' (*GA* 116). Halo, whose judgement is stable, sees
immediately that Vance 'was trying to do a masterpiece according to
the new recipe' and that he was in danger of 'sacrificing his individuality
to a fashion or school' (*GA* 101). At the end of the novel Vance in
New York reads a review of *Colossus* containing an assessment of his
oeuvre and the criticism that 'it was a pity . . . that so original a writer
had been influenced by the fashion of the hour' and realizes that Halo
had been right:

> 'Colossus' was not his own book, brain of his brain, flesh of his flesh, as it
> had seemed while he was at work on it, but a kind of hybrid monster
> made out of the crossing of his own imaginings with those imposed on
> him by the literary fashions and influences of the day. (*GA* 393)

At this point the bitterness of his artistic failure is overshadowed by
his regret that without a popular success Floss Delaney, like the fickle
public, would turn away from him. Ironically, the Stram set, whose
values Vance had rejected long before and who scorn his better work,
admire *Colossus* for 'like most artistic coteries they preferred a poor

work executed according to their own formula to a good one achieved without it' (*GA* 394)

The group of American expatriates encountered by Vance in France is contrasted with the group of British expatriates, to the detriment of the former. While the Americans are shown by Edith Wharton to be entirely lacking in taste and concerned only with the material, the British group, amongst whom Halo and Vance live for a time, although occupied by frugal and trivial interests 'yet managed by sheer community of sentiment to fit into the pattern of something big and immemorial' (*GA* 171). Vance is similarly impressed when he goes to England and recognizes the 'same sense of security and solidarity' (*GA* 274). London literary society which makes much of Vance reminds him of the old days at the Tarrants' but by now he knows that people in society 'were really indifferent to everyone and everything outside of their own circle' (*GA* 279). The 'genius' Octavius, idolized by this group, who is forever talking about his masterpiece but who never finds time to write it, is satirized by Edith Wharton in order to highlight the prevailing literary humbug, easily recognized by her hero.

While Vance consciously rejects false values in art and unconsciously adopts some fashionable approaches to the novel, he is never influenced by his admirers into accepting their valuation of him as, for example, Keniston, Betton and Gisburn are. His fans either are obviously frivolous women or are more concerned with the epithets they find to apply to his work than with the work itself. After his readings in London he thinks back to all those who had praised him without discernment: 'How his visions had dwindles under their touch – how he hated them for admiring him for the wrong reasons, and despised himself for imagining that their admiration was worth having!' (*GA* 292).

Domestic and social life combined with a time of international crisis to provide a new angle on the artist in relation to his society in *A Son at the Front* (1922). In previous works she had posed independence and individualism against the stable backgrounds of established society, whether the older orders of Europe and Old New York or the newer ethos of provincial America. Here the context is one of disorder – of expatriate life and loyalties, of changing ideas, of war. Campton, the artist, no longer young himself and devoted father of a young man, of settled habits in life and with an established reputation in art, provides a different perspective on the artist's perennial problem: while he is separated from most of humanity by his special nature and needs he cannot withdraw from society or be exempt from normal anxieties. The paradox for the artist at time of war lies in the fact that while he is part of the social upheaval and shares the suffering he is unlike most people in that his work becomes superfluous and he is largely useless and peripheral:

> I was meant to paint pictures in a world at peace, and I should have more respect for myself if I could go on unconcernedly doing it, instead of pining to be in all the places where I'm not wanted, and should be of no earthly use. (*SF* 189)

Through presenting the dilemma of her particular artist, Edith Wharton dramatizes what she herself felt living in Paris during the war: that 'the world in which men lived at present was one in which the word "art" had lost its meaning' (*SF* 128). By focusing on the problems of a particular individual at a particular moment in time, Edith Wharton makes the general point, important in her other fiction about the artist, that the artist, no less than any other member, is part of the society in which he lives and cannot avoid being affected by changes within it.

The central interest of *A Son at the Front* lies in John Campton's change of attitude towards the war and his son's involvement in it. He moves from a point where he refuses to accept that his son, born by chance in France to American parents, need be involved in the fighting and does his utmost to keep him away from the front to a point where he secretly longs for his son to insist on being relieved of his safe job and sent to the front. Campton's attitudes toward art and life are also changed: he feels that 'at a stroke, his only two reasons for living were gone: since the second of August he had no portraits to paint, no son to guide and to companion' (*SF* 128). In his changed world, he reassesses the way he has previously lived his life as a being apart:

> Well, perhaps after all the sin for which he was now atoning in loneliness was that of having been too exclusively an artist, of having cherished George too egotistically and self-indulgently, too much as his own most beautiful creation. If he had loved him more humanly, more tenderly and recklessly, might he have not put into his son the tenderness and recklessness which were beginning to seem to him the qualities most supremely human? (*SF* 176)

The war not only shakes Campton's private world and his beliefs but lead him to consider society as a whole and the meaning and pattern of history:

> All civilizations had their orbit; all societies rose and fell. Some day, no doubt, by the action of that law, everything that made the world livable to Campton and his kind would crumble in new ruins above the old . . .

Campton, brushing up his history, remembered the great turning points of progress, saw how the liberties of England had been born of the ruthless discipline of the Norman conquest, and how even out of the hideous welter of the French Revolution and the Napoleonic wars had come more freedom and a wiser order. The point was to remember that the efficacy of the sacrifice was always in proportion to the worth of the victims; and there at least his faith was sure. (SF 194)

(This optimistic point of view belongs to Edith Wharton's pre-war position from which she could assert that the cruelty of Richelieu was justified by the resulting order and stability he gave society: the death of her young friend Ronald Simmons – to whom she dedicated A Son at the Front – and the state of postwar society altered her objective view of the value of sacrifice and that the movement of society in Europe was towards progress.) As the war continues, Campton's views change and he no longer sees war as a regenerative force. Edith Wharton shows her artist on the one hand drawn into a closer relationship with society than he had ever had and, on the other, even more alienated by reason of his unique vision of reality:

He caught himself once more viewing the details of the scene in terms of his trade. River, pavements, terraces heavy with trees, the whole crowded skyline from Notre Dame to the Pantheon, instead of presenting themselves in their bare reality, were transposed into a painter's vision. And the faces around him became again the starting-point of rapid incessant combinations of line and colour, as if the visible world were once more at its old trick of weaving itself into magic designed. The reawakening of this instinct deepened Campton's sense of unrest, and made him feel more than ever unfitted for a life in which such things were no longer of account, in which it seemed a disloyalty even to think of them. (SF 221)

Because the artist according to Edith Wharton has an instinct for and a trained perception of beauty and harmony in the world, he is particularly vulnerable to disruption and chaos, and his sense of a split between his inner world and the actual world becomes more acute. For Campton, the artist's dual nature becomes a special problem rather than a source of strength. Edith Wharton shows other characters torn from their context by war, but Campton as a symbol of the Artist as well as the Father is seen to be particularly uprooted. In a world where practical values are the only possible ones, where the instinct to 'carry on' keeps people sane, the artist is at a disadvantage.

During one of the period when Campton regains his ability to work, he is drawn into a group of Americans which surrounds his son, George's, mistress, Mrs Talkett. Although Campton looks at these people 'through the cloud of his art' and 'impartially', Edith Wharton presents them with some savagery while ostensibly retaining Campton's impartial point of view:

> The high priestess of the group was Mme. de Dolmetsch, with Harvey Mayhew as her acolyte. Mr Mayhew was still in pursuit of Atrocities: he was in fact almost the only member of the group who did not rather ostentatiously disavow the obligation to 'carry on'. But he had discovered that to discharge this sacred task he must vary it by frequent intervals of relaxation. He explained to Campton that he had found it to be 'his duty' to rest; and he was indefatigable in the performance of his duty. (*SF* 229)

Campton tries to persuade himself and his friend, Daltrey, that he is justified in mixing with people who've decided, 'to forget the war, to ignore it, to live as if it were not and never had been' for a certain number of hours each day, and give 'little "war dinners" followed by a quiet turn at bridge' (*SF* 235). But the lack of American response to the sinking of the *Lusitania* seemed to Campton 'the ironic justification of the phase of indifference and self-absorption through which he had just passed' (*SF* 255) and he is unable to go back to the Talkett group or continue painting. Having lived in Paris throughout the war and been the centre of several war charities, and having toured the front with Walter Berry to deliver supplies and assess needs, Edith Wharton was understandably unable to portray impartially those who went on 'dancing and flirting and money-making on the great red mounds of the dead'.

However torn by emotion and dislocation, the artist's creative imagination remains immutably within him and liable to surface. Campton is suddenly struck by the graceful lines of his son's mistress and he begins to paint her:

> His first stroke carried him out of space and time, into a region where all that had become numb and atrophied in him could expand and breath. Lines, images, colours were again the sole facts . . . (*SF* 229)

Even at time of anxiety, his inspirations may take hold: when George returns to the front after recovering from his wound, Campton's emotions and suffering become the birth-pangs of a painting:

> As sometimes happened to him, the violent emotions of the last twenty-four hours had almost immediately been clarified and transmuted into vision. He felt that he could think contentedly of George if he could sit down at once and paint him.
>
> The picture grew under his feverish fingers – feverish and yet how firm! He always wondered anew at the way in which, at such hours, the

inner flame and smoke issued in a clear guiding radiance. He saw – he saw; and the mere act of his seeing seemed to hold George safe in some pure impenetrable medium. (*SF* 386)

George is immortalized in his father's painting but dies just as America finally enters the war and the tide is turned against the Germans. The day the first regiments from America march through Paris, Campton finally reconciles his work as an artist with a world in which it had come to seem pointless: he understood for the first time, 'he who had served Beauty all his days – how profoundly, at certain hours, it may become the symbol of things hoped for and things died for' (*SF* 410). As he watches the badly trained Americans march, 'his sorrow burst up in him in healing springs' and he is able to return to work:

> Now he felt the inspiration and the power returning, and he began to spend his days among the young American officers and soldiers . . . going about with them, and then hurrying home to job down his impressions. . . . His whole creative faculty was curiously, mysteriously engrossed in the recording of the young faces for whose coming George had yearned. (*SF* 412–3)

Campton comes to terms with grief and loneliness through his sense of the 'elemental quality' of grief that 'awful sense it communicated of a whirling earth, a crumbling Time, and all the cold stellar spaces yawning to receive us' (*SF* 422). Like Vance Weston, Campton feels a part of himself at one with the universal, and he comes to accept that through all his moods of despair and longing for his son 'ran the life-giving power of a reality embraced and accepted' (*SF* 423). He may often feel alienated from the society he lives in but he is inevitably part of it, and because he is what Claudia Day called 'the imperfect vehicle of the cosmic emotion' and must therefore convey that emotion from the 'republic of the spirit' to the actual world, he must understand that world and abide by its rules.

Edith Wharton's fiction about the artist from 1899 until the end of her life explores themes common to all her fiction and, indeed, to her non-fiction: the struggle between individual will and social codes; the need to balance the inner world of the imagination with the actual world; the obligation to have absolute standards of taste in social groups swayed by fashion; the necessity for order in private lives which requires compromise. The lesson Edith Wharton's individual must learn is that he or she has to make do with the actual world, with marriage, with society, with the petty irritations of everyday life, while never losing sight of the ideal, and for the artist with his heightened imagination that lesson is particularly hard: 'Life is not a matter of abstract principles, but a succession of pitiful compromises with fate, of concessions to old traditions, old beliefs, old tragedies, old failures' (*GA* 415). Edith Wharton shows the artist's's problems in balancing his inner and outer lives as being common to humanity but exacerbated because it is the artist's privilege and affliction to be more at home in the world of the imagination than in the real world. She sees order as a solution to the artist's difficulties in living in the ordinary world as much as it is a basis for his art: the creative artist's experience as a human being in society must be regulated by the same precepts which regulate its expression in his work.

Extracts from Edith Wharton's Notebook 1913

The extracts from Edith Wharton's notebook have been grouped in the following way: (a) ideas for plot or character; (b) short descriptions of scenery and characters and their feelings; (c) phrases, sentences or aphorisms, sometimes attached to a character; (d) paragraphs of narrative; (e) quotations; (f) sentences of dialogue or monologue; (g) sentences or paragraphs about literature or writing.

(a)   p. 2: In his liaison with Mrs R they take every risk, and are never found out; till it is all over, & he is giving her a last kiss, perfunctory on his side, resigned on hers – when the husband comes in –
Silmore
He is taken up by a patron who pays for his education (or gets him a scholarship?), & is then sent abroad, & expected to 'make good' in a year (or two?) by writing a book. Of course he doesn't – he hasn't yet anything to say & is thought a failure.

p. 7: Rose Ledwith seems to have literary feeling, & to laugh as much as anyone at the hack work she had to do; yet when she finally gets a chance to write as she pleases, she becomes conventionally sentimental and platitudinous – talks of 'artistry', 'deftness' 'daintiness' etc etc.
Uncle Horace
Dick Thaxter's father (clergyman) dies young, & his mother is much guided and influenced by a portentous brother – a vast 'pulido' void, with pompous & impressive manners, meticulous habits & an elaborately organized machinery for doing nothing – who shirks all responsibility about Dick, but manages to impress Mrs. T to the end – even after his incompetence has ruined her and her son.

p. 24: On the brink of losing all Dick's money for him, Uncle Horace gives him an immense 'enlarged' photograph of himself in a handsome frame – Horace himself *looks like an enlarged photograph* he had a large showy uninhabited face, as blank as a ballroom by daylight.

p. 27: A glittering shower swept the landscape.

(b) p. 1: Night on the river – Stars reflected between the black reflections of the poplars. The late red moon rising on the sea. Autumn. The end.

Rose

Now and then he saw the buried cities in her eyes.

p. 4: Carmen

She had crescent-shaped eyes – the lower lids curving slightly upward, & the corners of the upper drooping over it, & giving her an odd exotic look, as though she saw blue temples on yellow rivers.

p. 25: Dick in his misery, when his unhappy love obscures his art, Carmen Bliss has the small hard head of a Roman empress, Silmore gives Dick Baudelaire & Verlaine – beseeches him not to form a connection & Dick, to his amusement, discovered that the sophisticated S. thinks him still 'vierge' & probably *is* himself.

p. 29: Carmen Bliss's eyes were dark brown, with veined lids which seemed to be lined with onyx.

p. 36: Her fountain hair bubbled up with a young abundance over her eager head.

(c) p. 3: There is in the beginning of every relation between two people germ of [changed to 'hint of'] what is to destroy it – some little sign which is the clue to all that is coming afterward.

p. 4: Mrs [Birnam, in pencil] had happy originalities in dress wh. had no match in her ideas.

p. 11: [Rose's thoughts on Dick's passion passing] she had interested him mentally only as long as she attracted him physically.

p. 14: Levick says: – What an appalling thing literature has become now that clergymen's daughters have taken to writing about fauns!

p. 15: *Levick*

The measure of a character is in the nature of its dislikes. The man who hates people for being dull, ~~ugly or unhappy~~ [sic], has a narrower imagination than the man who hates people for being mean, venal & cruel, & is consequently nearer the dullness he despises.

p. 17: *Levick*

The worst thing about women is that if a man doesn't go on being in love with them forever they always think he never was from the first; & that necessitates a lot of retrospective talk – which of course does no good.

p. 19: There with her back to Giogione's Venus, sat Carmen Bliss, manicuring her nails.

p. 21: *Rose*
She wanted all the sea & all the night to come into their little room
. . .

p. 28: [Dick's feelings about Rose] She differed only in this generous largeness of view from the average pretty woman who clogs the wheels of progress.

p. 29: Marriage is like the ciborium that holds the Host in Catholic churches. The vessel is not sacred in itself but what it contains consecrates it. And so with marriage: it is consecrated by what it contains – patience, tenderness, disappointment, the birth and death of children, the planning and working together and the dreaming & despairing apart.

p. 36: The *impresario* –
Every word he spoke seemed to slap one on the back.

p. 35: Levick says to Rose (the last works of the book?) By the time you're forty people will begin to fall in love with you – & you'll end as a witty old woman with a reputation for epigram.

(d) [*Most of the passages of narrative are concerned with writing and therefore appear in section (g)*]
p. 22: Dicky, as he advanced in life began to discover that, although he enjoyed many of the things that other boys did, it was almost always for a different reason, & one they couldn't see if he tried to explain it.

p. 24: Dicky never thought of little girls with the contempt wh. he afterwards learned to be the customary attitude of infancy; but he frequently did not think of them at all.

p. 33: Dick, coming back, saw suddenly, with a fresh acuity of vision, her face so worn and diminished, under the bright imperishable hair.

p. 34: she knew the deceitful sweetness of drugged sleep, & the birth-agony of the reawakening to the truth.

(e) [*There are quotations from Hakluyt, Apuleius, Dante, Goethe, and an unacknowledged French source.*]

                              he
(f) p. 6: 'Call it a novel' Ralph [sic] gaily conceded to the remonstrance of his attendant genius; & a flash of irony made him add: 'It's only the label under which poetry sells nowadays!'

p. 31: Carmen says: 'I don't see why Paul thinks I'm extravagant. I'm wearing last years's sables.'

(g) p. 3: His verbal memory was not good, but the great things he read left a wall of fire in his brain.

He could now name his visions as they passed, & bid them pause & give themselves up to him (& lift the veil from their faces) The girl who is not in love with him reads to him divinely the poetry he has written to another woman.

p. 3: Waking every morning was like opening a new volume in the wonderful book he was reading.

p. 6: [Typed on a piece of paper stuck into the notebook, written on side in red 'Keep for Man of Genius']

He lingered on, watching his purpose take shape as the landscape below him moulded itself beneath the moon. Never before had his vision attained such precision in ecstasy: he had the distinct sense of having reached a new stage in the creative process. What was growing before him was not a poem; as it gathered outline & volume he saw it as a more solid rendering of life than had ever before emerged from his nebulous sensations. It was to be a novel – it one must restrict within any of the given formulas such a rich & complex presentment of experience as he now felt germinating within him! But the formula, after all, exited merely for the artist's convenience, was no more than the sheath through which the perfect flower was to break at its destined moment – Call it a novel etc.

p. 7: That sense of power wh. comes in long vigils, & in ardent incommunicable hours.

p. 11: The reading of a 'live' book always opened his eyes anew to the visible world. He saw with fresh precision the details of scenery, the meaning of faces, the colour of words; as though it were sometimes necessary that literature should bring him back to life, just
                        led
as, at other times life ~~brought~~ [sic] him to literature.

p. 13: The fascination of newly-conceived characters whom the writer is just beginning to know, & is perpetually making fresh discoveries about – Writing the first chapters of a new book is always like a love-affair.

[The popular novelist]

His art consisted in making the easy passages of his work so conspicuous that the hard ones – the ones he couldn't do – were overlooked.

            Levick
p. 15: ~~Homer Noyes~~   [sic]

The brilliant Socratic encyclopedic old man – a raté critic & hack journalist – who wakens Richard's literary consciousness, develops and stimulates him: & then cannot forgive him for being a creative artists & achieving the expression the other has always failed to attain.

p. 16: Rose Ledwith has the hyper sensibility, the over-exquisite-ness of perception, the too-prompt 'emotivity' – wh. are apt to be found with a certain kind of distinguished talent; Thaxter had the cool
~~stronger~~ [sic] command of all his aesthetic reactions wh. is the
    belongs
~~prerogative of~~ [sic] to genius. she spends in feeling (aesthetically & emotionally) what he finds full outlet for in expression. The difference between the amateur nurse and the surgeon. Genius is the greatest dérivatif of life – the only thing that saves one from the horrors of being intelligent.

p. 20: It seemed to Dick that to all the people about him words were mere domestic utensils, the pots and pans of their mental kitchens.

p. 22: Sometimes reading a single phrase was like entering into an immense temple.

p. 23: It seemed to him that literature contained all art and all beauty: that it was Greece & Egypt, & the utmost mountain solitudes: the evocative power of words gave him an awed sense of the supernatural.

p. 26: Levick says
Life-experience – yes, of course the novelist needs them: the more the better; though it's surprising how far a little can be made to go. The main thing is that it should come of itself. It's no more use to 'get up' experience than to 'get up' local colour. If it's acquired for literature it's of no use to literature. If it's in your nature to go about the streets with a monkey & handorgan, or to join the Camorra, or live with the cannibals, go & do it – but if what you really crave is home-life in a sanitary suburb, do *that* – a good novel's just as likely to come out of one as the other.

Scenario of *Literature*, with four facsimile pages

Facsimile of scenario of *Literature* (pages 2 and 3) as they appear in Edith Wharton's notebook.

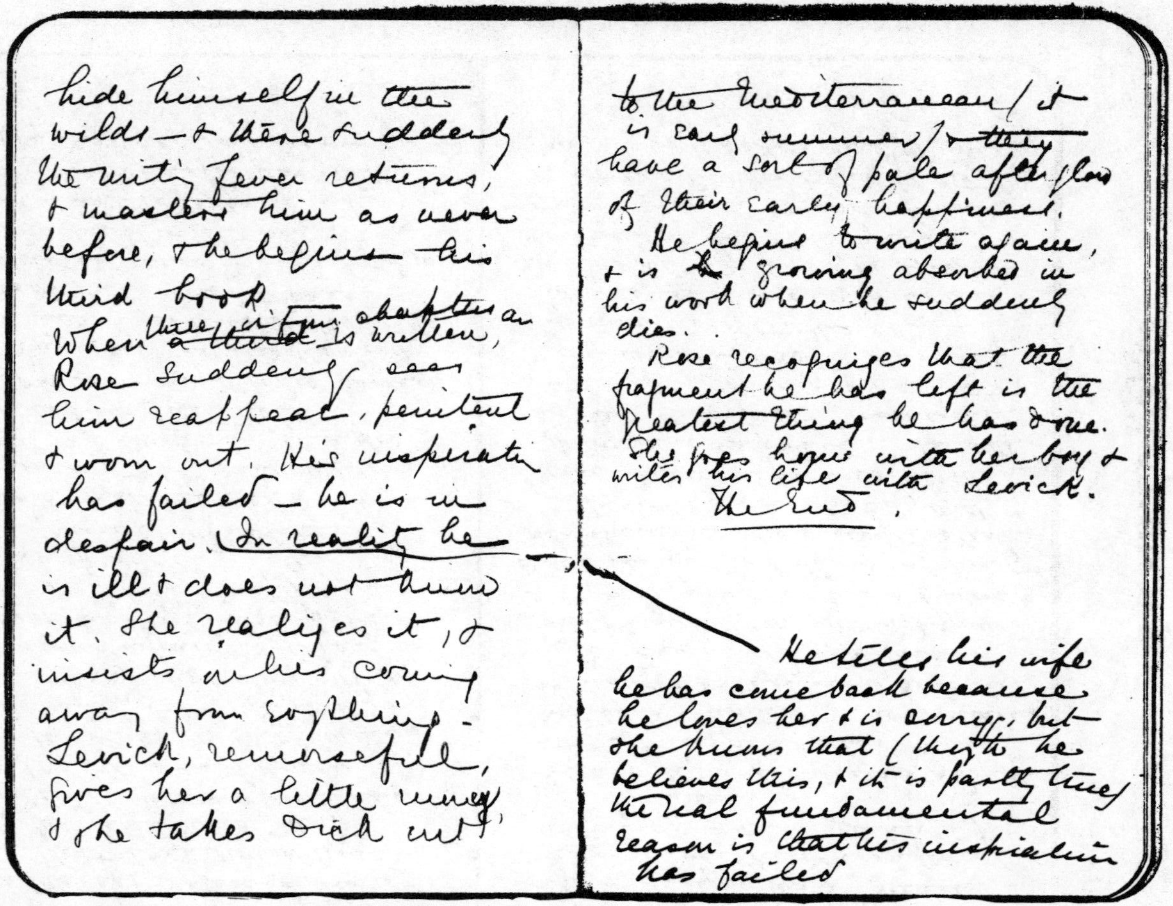

[The final draft ends at a point about three-quarters of the way down page four – marked with an asterisk.]

Literature.   Scenario.

(1st chapter already written)

Dick goes to school at 12 –

His father dies that year. Scene during his father's illness, when Mr Thaxter tries to tell him that he has never 'believed', & Mrs Thaxter, gathering up all our courage, says: 'your father is delirious', & puts Dick out of the room.

A few days later, edifying death-bed scene, Mr Thaxter scarcely conscious, clergyman praying, Mrs Thaxter reading psalms, Dick brought in – & sees his father die in the odour of orthodoxy.

(Several years afterward he taxes his mother with this, & she, though sincerely believing in the death-bed scene, which she had got up herself, nevertheless admits with tears that there were times when her husband 'had doubts.')

Mr Thaxter's library: very little theology, & no speculative or scientific books: Dick now understands why. His father was afraid, & tried to shut his eyes and stop his ears, & 'do his duty as a parish priest'. (All his wife's family, of whose wordly experience he, a shy unwordly person, stood somewhat in awe, though themselves thoroughly areligious, would have been scandalized beyond measure if he had renounced the priesthood, would have considered him to be 'unfrocked' (they didn't in the least know what it meant), & would have charged him withing bringing disgrace on his wife – though they 'never could understand dear Janet's marrying a clergyman.'

———

Uncle Wayne and Uncle Horace are left his guardians & his mother's trustees, & he remains at school & then goes to Harvard.

Already his 2 uncles have shrunk considerably in size, & he wonders more and more whn his father (whose superiority over them he had instinctively felt, even as a child) shd have been impressed by their 'business capacity.' Uncle Horace shifts the responsibility on Uncle Wayne & goes to live abroad, returning only for short visits. Uncle Wayne seems more and more muddled up in vague speculations, & the Thaxters' income is reduced & Dicky is worried about the future. But his uncle put him off with vague answers, & Mrs Thaxter begs him not to press the matter, out of regard for Grandma Boole & 'our of respect for his father's wishes'.

Book II

He completes Harvard, & during his last year writes his play. Reads it at Cleaver's studio, where Inez Clay takes a fancy to him & announces her intention of appearing in it. Cleaver, ardently convinced of Dick's genius, finances the production.*

Play total failure. Dick learns almost same time his own money almost gone, & is confronted by obligation to repay Cleaver. In talk, the latter lets slip that not he but his sister, Mrs Spofford Birnam (a good deal older) has 'put up' the money. Dick, aghast, goes to tell her of his difficulty & to thank her. – The scene, to his dismay, turns to sentiment, & he doesn't know how to escape. Brief liaison, wh. he tries to save from grotesqueness by poetizing it – but she is a 'psuedo-cult figure' & bores him, & is jealous & silly, & finally reminds him of his debt – & it is all sordid and shabby. At length she grows ashamed of the part she has played, & (his mother dying – or perhaps Grandma B?) he repays the money, & they are having a quiet scene of goodbye, that seems to retrieve the meanness of the episode – when, just as Dick is kissing her before leaving, Spofford Birnam comes in & surprises them.

About the same time a dilettantish person named Edwin Silmore, who has come across Dick in the Cleaver-Birnam pseudo–'artistic' set (& is one of its high-priests) proposes to Dick to send him abroad for a year (or two?) to travel, study & write a 'great book'. Silmore knows that Dick is very poor (his capital has mostly gone in repaying to Mrs Birnam the advance on the play), & that he has been trying to face going into business or getting a job on a paper.

He is drunk with joy at Silmore's offer, but after the scene with Julia Birnam & her husband (who threatened divorce – & is furious with everybody because he has 'found out', when all he asked was <u>not</u> to) he does not know whether he ought to stay & 'see it through'. – Finally, at the last moment, he decides to accept Silmore's offer & fly realizing that if he stayed, & possibly had to marry Mrs Birnam, it wd. destroy his talent, his life, everything.

Wonder-year in Europe. He had seen something, in New York, of a charming, original girl, Rose Ledwith, who writes <u>all</u> the articles in a cheap magazine (stories, travel, science etc) – she <u>is</u> the magazine. They strike up a Bohemian friendship & have good times together.

During his wandering abroad, he runs across her, over for the first time, on a hard-earned holiday. A day or two later she hears that the Editor of her magazine has gone bankrupt, & the whole thing has collapsed. She has had to borrow money for the trip, & she is left high & dry. He helps her out, & they have a few days together, when he very nearly yields to her attraction, but realizes the utter impossibility & flies. She goes home.

He returns to N.Y. after his year (or two?) & is eagerly hailed by Silmore & the expectant group. But he has written no.hing – hasn't an idea in his head. It is fallow-time with him, & they none of them understand it. Reports come that he has been seen travelling with a pretty woman (poor Rose), the story grows, & he is pictured to poor, shocked (& essentially conservative) Silmore as having spent his time in 'idleness & debauchery'. General chill. Dick turns against the whole artificial little group & strikes out in the big world of journalism & hack scribbling. He gets an unexpected chance as assistant ed. of a new magazine, makes a success of it, & runs again across Rose Ledwith, desperately in need of help. He publishes one or two of her stories, to help her (& against his conscience) & she suddenly gets to take herself seriously, & is offended when he refuses a third and further story, & finally tells her she doesn't know how to write. – He is distressed at her distress, & moved & charmed by her. At the same time he gets the dramatic criticism of a newspaper, & shortly after is made editor of the magazine. He now has a salary, & he marries Rose.

Suddenly, at the end of the year, the passion to write comes over him. He is discontented & miserable in his work, does it less well, quarrels with the proprietors of the magazine, & packing up, goes off to the country to write. Rose & he have a hard year. Then her boy is born, his book comes out & is a success, & everything smiles again. There is friction now & then between him & his wife as to her work, wh. she still takes seriously.

All through these years (ever since he left Harvard, & especially during his years of journalism & magazine work) he has been immensely under the influence of Caspar Levick, a strange Jew, a raté critic & hack journalist, with an amazing mind – a genius without creative faculty. Levick has sustained him through his deepest discouragements, developed, guided, matured him. He does not think much of Dick's book, but he says: 'Since it's a success, make the most of it, go to London & see people who are doing the same kind of thing – etc.' Dick goes, leaving Rose (but urged by her to do so), & once in Europe has a wildly triumphant few months in London & Paris, staying much longer than he had meant & spending much more money. – He runs across a strange girl, Carmen Bliss, whom he had met in Dresden on his previous trip (when Silmore sent him.) On that occasion he had met in Dresden a preposterous youth, Bowler Bush (son of the old sexton at Tryan), a boy in whom Mr Thaxter had interested himself, & who had got, in consequence, some sort of education, gone west; worked at every kind of job – & who suddenly turns up in Dresden 'personally conducting' a party of crude bewildered tourists from the uttermost Western town where he, Bush, happened to have been in business. – When Dick meets him he instantly suggests introducing him to the 'good-lookers' of the party, & Dick, amused at the adventure (but chiefly at Bowler Bush himself) is thrown for a day or two with these blank helpless creatures, goes on excursions with them, etc. One of the girls, Carmen Bliss, is attracted to him in an odd aggressive way, attempts to flirt crudely, then lapses into sulky disdain, amuses him & then bores him – & he thinks no more of her. – Now, on his return to England, he meets one day at a 'smart' house, a brilliant creature addressed as 'Princess' in whom he recognizes Carmen Bliss. She has married an Italian prince, & has become beautiful, intelligent & commanding. He is amazed & fascinated, she is drawn to thim, & invites him to stay in the country. He has a dizzy week, during wh. Rose is forgotten, a great chapter of a new book written, everything swept away by an overwhelming passion wh. he supposes to be shared. Then a smart party of people arrive, with a 'royalty' & a number of literary & artistic celebrities – & Dick sees himself ignored, forgotten, & finally almost asked to leave, as his room is needed. A desperate month in London follows.

He goes home, finds Rose ill & unhappy (she has heard the story) & tries to continue his novel. But he can do nothing.

Period of struggle & readjustment. He finally finishes his book – infinitely finer than the last, but does not sell nearly as well. Dick suddenly finds that Levick, who has remained his greatest source of strength has become bitterly & resentfully jealous, not of his temporary success, but of his really great achievement. – The following winter the Thaxters go to N.Y., & Dick begins a third book, & goes out in society a little. Rose does not go out, because she can't afford it. They live in a suburb, & she is brave & gay, because she had made up her mind that Dick is <u>worth it</u> – worth all she can do for him. – alternating moods on his part, but on the whole they are happier than for some time past.

The Princess turns up in N.Y. she is down on her luck, has less money, has come to N.Y. to see about business matters.

Meets Dick, finds him a celebrity, & tries to get him back. He resists, then yields – they have a stormy violent return of passion.

Levick discovers it & in a moment of bitterness tells Rose. It is more than she can bear. She reproaches Dick, makes 'a scene' (the first), & drives him wild. He goes back to the Princess, then is disgusted with both women, furious with himself, & ashamed, & goes off somewhere to hide himself in the wilds – & there suddenly the writing fever returns, & masters him as never before, & he begins his third book. –

When three or four chapters are written, Rose suddenly sees him reappear, penitent & worn out. His inspiration has failed – he is in despair. He tells his wife he has come back because he loves her & is sorry, but she knows that (though he believes this, & it is partly true) the real fundamental reason is that his inspiration has failed. In reality he is ill & does not know it. She realizes it, & insists on his coming away from everything. Levick, remorseful, gives her a little money, & she takes Dick out to the Mediterranean (it is early summer) & then have a sort of pale afterglow of their early happiness.

He begins to write again, & is growing absorbed in his work when he suddenly dies.

Rose recognizes that the fragment he has left is the greatest thing he has done. She goes home with her boy & writes his life with Levick.

<u>The End</u>

Chapter Summaries for *Literature*,
with four facsimile pages

Robt. *Literature*
Book I.

Chap I. Dick's first encounter with words. "O absalom:"

Chap II. The first kiss. Bowles Bush. Dick's impressions of his father. Reactions to nature, beauty - again the influence of words. First attempt at expression.

Chap III. School. Called home by his father's illness. The same stamp of confusion. Submissions of his I.-last-day Dick is tempted in business interest death. last scene.

Chap V. Begins to resent misusing result of projects, to take

Chap VI. Measure of work. Part of Literar. passion. Poems in school. magazine.

Chap VII. His misfortunes

Book II. Oct. 23 -

III Dick reads the freshn of Theoriented "cl-Clearers studies. Present Suzy Clay, Aunt Chancey, Mr Stafford Bowman + Caspar Derick (who is an old friend of Paris.)

Chap VIII. The play tacitly forbid, in all underbusy that Clearer "finances it. Reate life. Suzy Clay's adverse. Mrs Stafford. Bowman's interest + sympathy. A problem Chap.

that Mr Taylor had had "doubt." Dick for college. While Hat - a story or after he leave - all their money is lent. Uncle Wayne + Horace revealed to him as they really are.

13

14

Chap. XXXIX. Dick & Rose B. to the Mediterranean.

A fall after flow of their early bliss, & of their first travels. He begins trouble again. He seems much better.

Chap. XL. His work ahead

XL. Twin to the point of hallucination. He feels at last the ecstasy of complete human attainment.

Chap. XXXVI. He goes dim—moldering, &c.

Chap. XLI. Baptiste that his unfinished book is the real thing he has done.

Chap. XLII. He goes back with Territory, & writes his Territory's life will perish. Stories. "I want him to be a Painter."

+ goes off Thornville. He does not—elf has known what he is, in a hurry of inspiration he sets down all he has lived, which is to be the book, which is to be the book. Realized. He feels himself in full command of his powers.

Book VII. Act. 33 – 34.

Chap. XXXVII. His inspiration fails & he comes back, resistant & stunned. He does not know the reason—but it is because he is ill, & there are ties, & helpless & bitter. Then the little Rose comes & the Day marks in that they not live.

Chap. XXXVIII. Derick. Successful. He takes elaborate notation, & insists in Rose's death a little money & they shrink ahead.

Facsimile of pages 13 and 14 of the chapter summaries of *Literature*.

Literature

Book I

Chap I
Dicky's first encounter with words. 'O Absolom' –

Chap II
The first kiss. Bowler Bush. Dick's impressions of his father. Sensations of Nature, beauty – again the influence of words. First attempts at expression.

Chap III
School. Called home by his father's illness. Mr Thaxter's attempted confession. Interrupted by Mrs T. – Next day Dicky is brought in to witness orthodox death-bed scene.

Chap IV
Begins to scent mismanagement of property, & take measure of uncles. Growth of literary passion. Poems in school magazine.

Chap VI
His mother confesses that Mr Thaxter had had 'doubts'. Dick goes to college. While there – or the year after he leaves – all their money is lost. Uncle Wayne & Horace revealed to him as they really are.

Book II   aet 23

Chap VII
Dick reads 'The Duchess of Spartivento' at Cleaver's studio. Present Inez Clay, Rose Chancellor, Mrs Spofford Birnam & Caspar Levick (who is an old friend of Rose's).

Chap VIII
The play taken by Garbish on the understanding that Cleaver 'finances' it. Theatre life. Inez Clay advances. Mrs. Spoff. Birnam's interest & sympathy. A golden glow.

Chap IX
Production. Total failure. Despair. How shall he pay? Discovers that Mrs Birnam has advanced the money, not Cleaver. Goes to thank her. Sentimental scene. He is in the toils.

Chap X
The first 'love-affair'. Dick's misery. The pseudo-culture of Mrs Birnam's set. His longing to get away from it all. He runs across Rose Chancellor every now & then – also Levick, whose talk makes him more & more sick of the people he is seeing & the life he is leading.

Chap XI
He is doing hack journalism (literary criticism etc) to try to pay off Mrs B. – He is thrown (in her group) with Edwin Silmore, the prophet of the pseudos – a rich 'kindly ass' who takes a great fancy to Dick.

Chap XII	Meanwhile the Birnam bondage grows daily more intolerable.
Aet. 24	Quarrels. Jealousy of Mrs B. (15 years older). Dick rebellious & bitter. At length Mrs B. grows ashamed of the part she has played, & – Grandma Boole having died about this time & left her grandson a legacy – Dick is suddenly able to pay his debt. The fact softens him, but he is as firmly resolved as ever to be free. Mrs B. understands & accepts this, & they say goodbye. As they are exchanging a last perfunctory kiss Birnam comes in & 'surprises' them.
Chap XIII	Dick's anguish. What must he do, what will be expected of him?
Aet. 25	He goes home & finds Silmore waiting for him. Silmore has come to offer him a 'wander year' in Europe (or two?). Dick's money has almost all gone in paying Brs B., & he had been facing the necessity of settling down to regular newspaper work, wh. he naturally loathes. Freedom & foreign lands are what he longs for – & to be with <u>real</u> natural people. But he feels he ought perhaps to await the issue of the Birnam situation. What will the husband do & – He dares not consult Silmore. He accepts the latter's offer & flies. Silmore is persuaded he will come back with 'a great book.'

Book III   Aet. 25–26

Chap XIV	The wonder-time in Europe begins.
Chap XV	Dresden. Bowler Bush. Carmen Bliss.
Chap XVI	Meets again Rose Chancellor, abroad on holiday.
Chap XVII	Rose Chancellor.
Chap XVIII	Rose Chancellor

Book IV   <u>Aet. 27–28</u>

Chap XIX	Back to Silmore & the pseudos – without a book. Dick sees that they regard him as a failure. He gives up everything (Rose, after the first shock, encouraging & believing in him) & they shut themselves up in the country in a tiny cottage. A hard year for Rose, a glorious one for Dick.
Chap XXIV	Their boy is born, & his novel finished. 'John Santorin'. Literary success.
Chap XXV Aet. 29–30	Levick alone does not think much of the book, but tells Dick to use the money he has made to go

abroad for two or three months, mix with men of letters in Paris & England, & open his eyes & ears. Rose approves, & he goes, leaving her & the boy behind.

Book V.   Aet. 30–32

Chap XXVI	Another wonder-time. London. Carmen Bliss again ('the Princess').
Chap XXVII	Dick & the Princess. He begins a new novel.
Chap XXVIII	Dick & the Princess – the disillusionment.
Chap XXIX	He goes home, & finds Rose has heard the story, & is very unhappy. Dick has stayed abroad much longer than he meant to, & spent more money. He tries to console Rose & to continue his novel. He cannot write. Difficult days.
Chap XXX	Period of struggle & readjustment. Dick finally finishes his book. It is much 'bigger' than the last, & is recognized by a few critics, but does not sell as well.
Chap XXXI	Dick, who has depended for a long time on Levick's encouragement & on his dauntless criticism, now sees a change in his friend, & discovers that Levick, himself without the gift of invention, has become bitterly & resentfully jealous of Dick's first great achievement (though indifferent to his popular success).
Chap XXXII	The Thaxters settle in a small house on the outskirts of N.Y. & Dick begins a third novel, & goes into society – the 'smart' & gay rather than the culture pseudos. Rose stays at home, as she can't afford the clothes. But she is brave & gay, & proud of Dick – she has made up her mind he is 'worth it'. Alternating moods on both sides, but on the whole they are happier than for some time.

Book VI   Aet 32

Chap XXXIII	The following winter the Princess turns up in N.Y. – She finds Dick a celebrity, & wants him again.
Chap XXXIV	They go off for a few days.
Chap XXXV	Levick discovers it, & in a moment of bitter rancour tells Rose. She reproaches Dick on his return, & makes 'a scene' (the first.) He is driven wild by her reproaches, goes back to the Princess, & is in turn disgusted by her vanity & vulgarity.

Chap XXXVI
He decides to
kill himself; &
at that moment
the thought of
a big book
comes to him
& he sits down
& writes the
scenario.

In the thick of this crisis he has a sudden phase of complete artistic detachment. The fever to write, the power of expression, return with unparalleled intensity. Furious & disgusted with his sentimental dilemma he flies both women & goes off to the wilds. He does not let Rose know where he is. In a frenzy of inspiration he sets to work on his third book, which is to be the greatest. He feels himself in full command of his genius.

Book VII   Aet. 33–34

Chap XXXVII   His inspiration fails & he comes back, penitent & discouraged. he does not know the reason – but it is because he is ill, & Rose sees this, & forgives and pities. His health grows worse, & the Drs. warn her that he may not live.

Chap XXXVIII   Levick, remorseful, sees their desperate situation & insists on Rose's accepting a little money & taking Dick abroad.

Chap XXXIX   Dick & Rose go to the Mediterranean. A pale afterglow of their early bliss, & of their first travels. He begins to write again. He seems much better.

Chap XL   His work absorbs him to the point of hallucination. He feels at last the ecstasy of complete attainment.

Chap XLI   He dies suddenly, & Rose recognizes that his unfinished book is the greatest thing he has done.

Chap XLII   She goes to America with her boy, & writes her husband's life with Levick. – she says of the boy: 'I want him to be a genius.'

Facsimiles of extracts from MS draft of *Literature*

89

to the higher influences, *he would* hardly have known how to get a hearing for his play; & here it was not only heard but appreciated, & actually, as it seemed, on the verge of production. His suddenly revived faith in old Rollins's *intelligence* became *comprehensive* enough to include old Rollins's sister, & he said to himself that Mrs Binham *was an extremely agreeable woman* & that he had been a *big* dolt not to notice it before, when they had met in Europe.

"You must come & see me some afternoon late. Mr Thaxter... *very late*..." "Oh, I haven't said goodbye to Miss Clay, or thanked her for her *marvellous* reading..." Mrs Binham, *floated off* showering italics to right & left, floated off in a dark shimmer of furs, with Leny Marsh at her elbow, & Dick's thoughts flew back to Miss Clay, still for him the central figure of the day. But the day, was

90

breaking up, & Miss Clay, dabbing powder
on her nose the reflected in the cracked surface of
a ~~tiny mirror~~ pocket-mirror, was
saying to one of the other young men: "Don't
be ~~afraid~~ so fresh — I've got a rehearsal."
Her lustrous eyes rested on
Dick, & she ~~let them~~ let him have
a long draught of them. When she looked
at him like that, how could he ask
her when she meant to speak to Jarvis?
He said to himself that he would stop at the
florist and send her roses ... But in the
mischief of the pause sign to him with the
general explosion of farewells.
    'I shan't forget, but you know I'm
awfully tied down all balled up with a rehearsal.
We bring out 'Mint Juleps' on the fifth.
But come round behind any night." She
glanced over her shoulder. "Rino Lanning —
I'll drop you at the office if you like."
    There was a burst of laughter at
the other end of the studio, in the shadow of
a small women-laden balcony wh. Rollins
had ... "... minstrels."

Facsimiles of extract from first typed draft of *Literature*

1.

LITERATURE.

Book I.

Chapter I.

The most decisive event of Richard Thaxter's ~~youth~~ *life* — though one ~~which is~~ unrecorded in his ~~voluminous and adroitly~~ *admirably* compiled Biography — occurred on a hot June Sunday, in his father's church at Tryan-on-Hudson.

Having early learned to submit to church-going as to one of the unintelligible laws which hem in a little boy's life, Richard Thaxter, by the age of seven, had ~~evolved a~~ *worked out* a simple method of minimizing its ~~troubles~~ *evils*. Securely fitted into the irregular recess formed by his mother's thin side and his grandmother Boole's cushioned outworks, propping his knees against the former, and *sinking* his head into the latter, surface, he stared up past ~~the~~ chancel and pulpit, and his father's fussy, flapping white presence, (it always gave him an odd feeling of embarrassment to look at his father in church) at the steep ~~beam~~ *brown* roof which had been jig-sawed into a carpenter's parody of *p*erpendicular Gothic. A swallow had once nested there, flitting in and out for a summer; and though the bird was gone and its nest removed (at the request of the grocer, who sat in the pew ~~under~~ *underneath* it) that particular corner of the groining still seemed to Dicky Thaxter full of the murmur and rustle of out-doors. In its music he lost

2.

himself, the delusion aided by the warm scent of his own
nest, which smelt of lettuce soap on his mother's side and
of camphor or sandal-wood (according to the season) on his
grandmother's.   He was not asleep, he was simply what is
called "being good"; a state of repose for his elders and of
s̶t̶r̶a̶n̶g̶e̶ drowsy ecstasy for himself.   Dicky never objected to
being good when he was comfortable, and there was nothing
better to do; and if you had had time to run your legs off
with the dogs after breakfast, it was comfortable enough to
curl up in the pew, with your head in your grandmother's
roundness, and think sleepy things about the place where the
swallow had been.   (It was a source of pride to Grandma Boole
that Dicky was always reported as being "less good" on the
Sundays when her rheumatism kept her from church.)

        Immersed in this state of beatitude, Dicky was never-
theless a̶l̶w̶a̶y̶s̶ aware of the progress of the service as a
burrowing animal may be of the passage of the daylight
overhead.   Some obscure sense of the lapse of time told him
when to lower his legs for the next hymn, and enabled him to
distinguish the gospel and epistle from the lessons;   and he
always knew when he could abandon himself to the final repose
of the sermon.   He was sure, therefore, that the sermon had
begun, and been several minutes in progress, before the thing
happened which, even there, on the spot, he obscurely felt to
be a great event, an event as great as could happen in anything so small as his life.

3.

"O Absalom, my son, my son Absalom, would God I
had died for thee, O Absalom, my son, my son!"

That was what happened - this rain of celestial syllables pouring down on him from heights higher than the swallow's
nest and the summer sky.   Words - just words joined together
and meaning something so simple that he could class the phrase
immediately with the familiar maternal reproach: "Oh, Dicky,
I do wish you hadn't done that!" or his father's sterner:
"My boy, I'm sure you've disobeyed me."   But he didn't care
a straw what the words meant: that had nothing to do with
it.   He simply noticed that they _were_ words; and that was
the great event.   He had noticed many things already: birds,
dogs, beetles, tadpoles, people's faces, the look of rooms
and the pictures on their walls.   But he had never noticed
words, or the sound of words joined together; and now the
wonder of the linked syllables seemed to catch his little
heart in a grasp of fire.   He shut his eyes and listened,
praying that his father would say them again.   But his
father's discourse ran on as usual, dull as a road if one
had to drive over it: (going to church always reminded Dicky
of taking a drive, because you couldn't jump out and touch
and taste the things you saw by the way.)   He listened in
vain, forgetting the lapse of time, forgetting to watch for
the "And now unto Him" for which he usually yearned with such
all-over pricklings of his impatient body; till suddenly
the walls of his niche collapsed, and he found himself preci-

Facsimiles of extract from second typed draft of *Literature*

Literature.

BOOK I.

I.

The most decisive event of Richard Thaxter's life—— though one unrecorded in his admirably compiled Biography—— occurred on a hot June Sunday in his father's church at Tryan-on-Hudson.

Having early learned to submit to church-going as to one of the unintelligible laws which hem in a little boy's life, Richard Thaxter, by the age of seven, had worked out a simple method of minimizing its evils. Securely fitted into the irregular recess formed by his mother's thin side and his grandmother Boole's cushioned outworks, propping his knees against the former, and sinking his head into the latter, surface he stared up past chancel and pulpit, and his father's fussy flapping white presence (it always gave him an odd feeling of embarrassment to look at his father in church) at the steep brown roof which had been jig-sawed into a carpenter's parody of Perpendicular Gothic. A swallow had once mated there, flitting in and out for a summer; and though the bird was gone and its nest removed (at the request of the grocer, who sat in the pew underneath it), that particular corner of the groining still seemed to Dicky Thaxter full of the murmur and rustle of out-doors. In its music he lost himself, the delusion aided by the warm scent of his own nest, which smelt of lettuce soap on his mother's side and of camphor or sandal-wood (according to the season) on his grandmother's. He was not asleep, he was simply what is called "being good"; a state of repose for his elders and of drowsy ecstasy for himself. Dicky never objected to being good when he was comfortable, and there was nothing better to do; and if you had had time to run your legs off

with the dogs after breakfast, it was comfortable enough to curl up in
the pew, with your head in your grandmother's roundness, and think
sleepy things about the place where the swallow had been. (It was a
source of pride to Grandma Boole that Dicky was always reported as bein
"less good" on the Sundays when her rheumatism kept her from church.)

Thus Immersed in ~~this state of~~ beatitude, Dicky was nevertheless
aware of the progress of the service as a burrowing animal may be of t
passage of the daylight overhead. Some obscure sense of the lapse of
time told him when to lower his legs for ~~the next~~ hymn, and enabled hi
to distinguish the gospel and epistle from the lessons; and he always
knew when he could abandon himself to the final repose of the sermon.
He was sure, therefore, that the sermon had begun, and been several
minutes in progress, before the thing happened which, even there, on t
spot, he obscurely felt to be a great event, an event as great as coul
happen in anything so small as his life.

            "O my son Absalom, my son, my son Absalom, would God I had
died for thee, O Absalom, my son, my son!"

            That was what happened— this rain of celestial syllables
pouring down on him from heights higher than the swallow's nest and th
summer sky. Words— just words joined together and meaning something
so simple that he could class the phrase immediately with the familiar
maternal reproach: "Oh, Dicky, I do wish you hadn't done that!" or h
father's sterner: "My boy, I'm sorry you've disobeyed me." But he
didn't care a straw what the words meant: that had nothing to do with
it. He simply noticed that they _were_ words; and that was the great
event. He had noticed many things already: birds, dogs, beetles, tadpoles, people's faces, the look of rooms and the pictures on their
walls. But he had never noticed words, or the sound of words joined t
gether; and now the wonder of the linked syllables seemed to catch his

ittle heart in a grasp of fire. He shut his eyes and listened, praying
hat his father would say them again. But his father's discourse ran on
.s usual, dull as a road if one had to drive over it: (going to church
.lways reminded Dicky of taking a drive, because you couldn't jump out
.nd touch and taste the things you saw by the way.) He listened in
-ain, losing his sense of time, forgetting to watch for the "And now
.nto Him" for which he usually yearned with such all-over pricklings of
.is impatient body; till suddenly the walls of his niche collapsed, and
.e found himself precipitated to his knees under the final "Life Ever-
.asting", which his father always pronounced as if it were the jam after
:he powder.

They were all at luncheon at the Rectory that Sunday (it was
:alled dinner on Sundays,. except when Uncle Horace came):Uncle Wayne
:itterick and Aunt Lucy, who had driven over from Brown Towers, their
·lace on the Hudson, and Uncle Horace Boole, who was staying with them,
.nd Aunt Elizabeth Kitterick, Uncle Wayne's elder sister, who lived just
·utside of Tryan, in a ginger-coloured house set on beautiful steep
;rass-banks that Dicky was positively forbidden to slide down (though he
.ight pick the raspberries in the garden if the gardener were there, and
:troke the cat if it were in Aunt Elizabeth's lap).

They were all there, and they all knew a great deal: they
:ould probably, any one of them, have told Dicky where his wonderful
·ords came from and why they were so wonderful. Uncle Wayne Kitterick
·as a small busy man with a brown face, scintillating eye-glasses and a
:ombative manner. He was always full of plans for improving and re-
.ressing things, and now and then Aunt Lucy (who was larger and slower)
.ad to say warningly: "Wayne, you'll wear yourself out", as Mrs.
:haxter did when Dicky bicycled too many times round and round the drive.
:ut Uncle Wayne went on just the same, denouncing "outrages" (which

Comparison of extract from MS draft of *Literature* with typed draft

posed receptivity to the higher influences, he would hardly have known how to get a hearing for his play; and here it was not only heard but appreciated, and actually, as it seemed, on the verge of production. His suddenly revived faith in old Rollins's intelligence became comprehensive enough to include old Rollins's sister, and he said to himself that Mrs. Birnam was an extremely agreeable woman, and that he had been a young dolt not to discern it when they had met in Europe.

"You must come and see me some afternoon late, Mr. Thaxter... very late... Oh, I haven't said good-bye to Miss Clay, or thanked her for her marvellous reading..." Mrs. Birnam, showering italics, floated off in a dark shimmer of furs, with Lorry Marsh at her elbow, and Dick's thoughts flew back to Miss Clay, still for him the central figure of the day. But the party was breaking up, and Miss Clay, dabbing powder on the nose reflected in the cracked surface of her gold pocket-mirror, was saying to one of the other young men: "Don't be fresh— I've got a rehearsal." Her lustrous eyes rested on Dick, and she let him have a draught of them. When she looked at him like that, how could he ask her when she meant to speak to Garbish? He said to himself that he would stop at the florist's and send her some roses... But on the threshold she paused to sign to him through the general explosion of farewells.

"I sha'n't forget; but you know I'm all balled up with rehearsals. We bring out 'Mint Julep' on the fifth. But come round behind any night." She glanced over her shoulder. "Rose Lansing— I'll drop you at the office if you like."

There was a burst of laughter at the other end of the room, in the shadow of a small worm-eaten balcony which Rollins had described as "the minstrel gallery" when "Art in the Home" had published carbon prints of his studio.

Edith Wharton's works referred to in the text with abbreviations used

Books

AA   *The Age of Innocence.* New York: Scribner's, 1970 (first publ. 1920).
BG   *A Backward Glance.* New York: Appleton-Century, 1934.
     The Buccaneers. New York: Appleton-Century, 1938.
     'The Bunner Sisters', in *Madame de Treymes and Others.* New York: Scribner's, 1970 (first publ. 1916).
     The Children. New York: Appleton, 1928.
CBS   *Collected Short Stories* Vol. II (ed. R.W.B. Lewis). New York: Scribner's, 1968.
CI   *Crucial Instances.* New York: Scribner's, 1899.
CC   *The Custom of the Country.* New York: Scribner's, 1956 (first publ. 1913).
DH   *The Decoration of Houses.* New York: W.W. Norton, 1978 (first publ. 1897).
     The Descent of Man and other Stories. New York: Scribner's, 1904.
     Ethan Frome. New York: Scribner's, 1970 (first publ. 1911).
FF   *Fighting France, from Dunkerque to Belfort.* New York: Scribner's, 1915.
FW   *French Ways and their Meaning.* New York: Appleton, 1919.
     The Glimpses of the Moon. New York: Appleton, 1922.
GA   *The Gods Arrive.* New York: Scribner's 1960 (first publ. 1932).
GI   *The Greater Inclination.* New York: Scribner's, 1899.
HWW   'The Hermit and the Wild Woman', in *Collected Short Stories* Vol. II (ed. R.W.B. Lewis) (first publ. 1908).

HM	*The House of Mirth*. Boston: Riverside Press, 1963 (first publ. 1905).
HRB	*Hudson River Bracketed*. New York: New American Library of World Literature, 1962 (first publ. 1929).
	'Human Nature', in *Collected Short Stories* Vol. II (ed. R.W.B. Lewis) (first publ. 1933).
IM	*In Morocco*. London: Macmillan, 1920.
ItB	*Italian Backgrounds*. New York: Scribner's, 1905.
ItV	*Italian Villas and their Gardens*. New York: Century, 1904.
LIT	*Literature*. Unpublished: in the Beinecke Library at Yale University. A manuscript note book, 69 pages of manuscript and two typescript drafts of the unfinished novel. (Refs Za25–28).
	Madame de Treymes and Others: Four novelettes. New York: Scribner's, 1970 (first publ. 1910, 1916).
	The Marne. New York: Appleton, 1918.
	The Mother's Recompense. New York: Appleton, 1925.
MF	*A Motor-Flight through France*. New York: Scribner's, 1908.
	Old New York: False Dawn (The forties); *The Old Maid* (The Fifties); *The Spark* (The Sixties); *New Year's Day* (The Seventies). New York: Appleton, 1924 (4 vols).
	The Reef. New York: Appleton, 1912.
SF	*A Son at the Front*. New York: Scribner's, 1924.
	Summer. New York: Harper & Row, 1980 (first publ. 1917).
	Tales of Men and Ghosts, in *Collected Short Stories* Vol. II (ed. R.W.B. Lewis) (first publ. 1910).
	The Valley of Decision. New York: Scribner's, 1902 (2 vols).
WF	*The Writing of Fiction*. New York: Scribner's, 1924.
	The World Over, in *Collected Short Stories* Vol. II (ed. R.W.B. Lewis) (first publ. 1936).
WWS	'Writing a War Story', in *Collected Short Stories* Vol. II (ed. R.W.B. Lewis) (first publ. 1919).

Articles

'William C. Brownell', *Scribner's Magazine* 84 (Nov. 1928), 596–602.

'Confessions of a Novelist', *Atlantic Monthly* 151 (Apr. 1933), 385–92).

CF   'The Criticism of Fiction', *Times Literary Supplement* 14 May 1914, 229–30.
            'A Cycle of Reviewing', *Spectator* 141 (23 Nov. 1928), supplement, 44.
            'Fiction and Criticism', unpublished, in the Beinecke Library, Yale. (Ref Za215).

GAN   'The Great American Novel', *Yale Review* n.s. 16 (July 1927), 646–56.
            'George Eliot', a review of Leslie Stephen's book, *Bookman* (May 1902).
            'Henry James in his Letters', *Quarterly Review* 234 (July 1920), 188–202.

LGNY   'A Little Girl's New York', *Harper's Magazine* 176 (Mar. 1938), 356–64.

PVF   'Permanent Values in Fiction', *Saturday Review of Literature*, 10 (38) (7 Apr. 1934), 603–4.

RP   'A Reconsideration of Proust', *Saturday Review of Literature*, 11 (15) (27 Oct. 1934), 233–4.

TMF   'Tendencies in Modern Fiction', *Saturday Review of Literature*, 10 (28) (27 Jan. 1934), 433–44.

VR   'The Vice of Reading', *North American Review* 177 (Oct. 1903), 513–21.

VF   'Visibility in Fiction', *Yale Review* n.s. 18 (Mar. 1929), 480–8.

Other Abbreviations Used

RWBL   R.W.B. Lewis, *Edith Wharton: A Biography*. New York: Harper & Row, 1975.

PL   Percy Lubbock, *Portrait of Edith Wharton*. London: Jonathan Cape, 1947.

Notes

Items listed in the Bibliography or in the Writings of Edith Wharton are referred to here in abbreviated form.

Sources of primary material
Edith Wharton papers Beinecke Library, Yale University.
Charles Scribner Sons archives; author files 1, boxes 1, 6, 7, 8, Firestone Library, Princeton University.
Edith Wharton, letters to Bernard Berenson, Villa I Tatti Library, Settignano, Florence.

Introduction

1. Goethe, letter to Wilhelm von Humboldt, 17 March 1832 (Goethe, 1958, p. 40), in which he is replying to Humboldt's request for further explanation of the creative process.

Chapter One

1. The quotation comes from Thomas Traherne, *The Vision*. It appears both on the title page of *The Writing of Fiction* and on the second page of her diary, 1924.
2. Vernon Lee (Violet Paget) was a friend of Edith Wharton whose encouragement Wharton acknowledged in *A Backward Glance* (p. 133) and to whom she dedicated *Italian Villas and their Gardens*.
3. The garden is now being restored.
4. Letter to Berenson dated March 1930 (I Tatti collection).
5. Letter to Berenson dated 6 Jan. 1923 (I Tatti collection).
6. Remark made to John Hugh-Smith cited in Lewis 1975, p. 435. The admiration was mutual: Lewis dedicated *Babbit* to Wharton.
7. Sybil Bedford, *Aldous Huxley*, Quartet Books, London, 1979, Vol. I *passim*.
8. The list is based on quotations and references to Lewis 1977.

Chapter Two

1. Unpublished article in the Edith Wharton collection in the Beinecke Library, Yale.

2. Daisy Terry, who married Winthrop Chanler, was a friend of Edith Wharton from youth.
3. Letter to W.C. Brownell 19 Sept. 1920 (Beinecke Library).
4. Letter to Bernard Berenson 4 Jan. 1911 (I Tatti collection).
5. Henry James, 'The Younger Generation', *Times Literary Supplement*, 2 Apr. 1914, 158.
6. Brown 1962, p. 67.
7. Lyde 1959, Ch. 3.
8. Poirier 1965, p. 216.
9. 'The Bunner Sisters', p. 227.
10. Unpublished article in the Edith Wharton collection in the Beinecke Library, Yale (Za 215).
11. See also 'The Great American Novel', pp. 646–56.

Chapter Three

1. Originally published as 'Confessions of a Novelist', *Atlantic Monthly*, April 1933, 385–92.
2. Cf. Goethe on creative productiveness: man may often be considered 'a vessel worthy to contain a divine influence' (*Conversations of Goethe*, in Goethe, 1958, p. 22).
3. This image reflects her interest in the work of Charles Darwin and in particular *Structure and Distribution of Coral Reefs*, Murray, London, 1842.
4. In one of Edith Wharton's notebooks in the Beinecke Library at Yale there are some jottings for a work to be called 'Magic', which is concerned with Mesmer and his ideas.
5. This quotation stands on the title page of *The Gods Arrive*. The title of the novel comes from Emerson's poem 'Give All to Love'. Lewis (1975, p. 502) comments 'The best thing about the book, one is tempted to say, is its title, from a poem by Emerson: "When half-gods go/The gods arrive".'
6. In a short story, 'Expiation' (in *The Descent of Man*), the Bishop of Ossining confesses that if only his book were to be denounced its circulation would increase and he would be able to fill the chantry window with the proceeds. Meanwhile his niece, who has written a novel with the title of Edith Wharton's childhood novel 'Fast and Loose', is advised to ask the Bishop to preach against it.
7. Halo is surprised when Vance calls it an old house: 'Well – after all everything is relative . . . Father's great-uncle Ambrose Lorburn built it, I believe . . . Say about 1830. Well, that *does* make it very nearly an old house for America, doesn't it? Almost a hundred years!' (*HRB* 55).
8. See also *WF*, 52, 142 and 165.
9. See also *GA*, 111, 117.

Chapter Four

1. In 1901 Edith Wharton completed two acts of a play of this name and an elaborate outline of the rest of the action. The plot is not the same as the novel outlined in this notebook.
2. She visited Dresden with Bernard Berenson for an ill-fated trip to Germany during the latter half of August 1913 (Lewis 1975, pp. 351–5).
3. Letter to Bernard Berenson 23 December 1912 (I Tatti collection).
4. The letters are held at the Firestone Library, Princeton.
5. Edith Wharton's divorce from Teddy in April 1913 publicly marked the culmination of years of strain and worry. Teddy's increasingly erratic behaviour over money and women since 1908 and his family's unhelpful attitude towards his mental health had taken its emotional toll on his wife. Henry James describes her in 1912 as 'Teddy's victim' and in a letter to Howard Sturgis refers to her marriage as an 'inconceivable thing'; Teddy he describes to Gaillard Lapsley as 'violent and scenic'. She writes to Berenson and his wife Mary about Teddy's health from April 1910: 'My husband has had a persistent neurasthenia for the last four or five months and it does not seem to improve.'
   From this time until May 1914 (more than a year after their divorce) she reports on Teddy and the exhaustion his behaviour and health bring to her. From a letter to Mary Berenson from Paris on 7 February 1913 when the Wharton marriage was reaching its end, we get some idea of what life over some years had been like:

> What I have been hearing lately, from America, and from Monte Carlo also, is so much wilder and worse that Ralph Curtis's sketch [related to Mrs Wharton by Mrs Berenson] seems much bowdlerized! My cousin has been here looking after my interests, and saw my husband at Monte Carlo leading a life he wouldn't describe to me except in gestures of disgust, and I couldn't have listened to it if he *had* – & friends and relations in America have been writing me on all sides that I must 'act'; so I hope something may soon be decently, silently and soberly arranged.
> I'm utterly tired out, but can't leave for another month probably.

Her estrangement from Teddy was a contributory factor in her break with America – though her fondness for European intellectual society, where Teddy was a misfit, was surely a factor in that estrangement. Many of their disagreements were, overtly, over the management of the house designed and built by Edith Wharton near Lenox, Massachusets, called 'The Mount', which they both loved but which was finally sold in 1912. In *A Backward Glance* she writes about 'The Mount': 'There for over ten years I lived and gardened and wrote contentedly, and should have doubtless ended my days there had not a grave change in my husband's health made the burden of the property too heavy' (*BG* 125). Edith Wharton never had another home in America, and she only visited it twice after 1912, once for her niece's wedding in 1913, and finally in 1923 to receive her honorary doctorate from Yale. She was further detached from her roots and her family by a quarrel with her favourite brother, Harry, in January 1913, which was never made up, although he too lived in Paris – as did her elder brother, Freddy, with whom she had never been on close terms.

Having no longer any immediate family or a husband, and living in a foreign country, Edith Wharton's friends became even more precious to her. In a letter to Bernard Berenson written just after the end of the war, this is clear; the letter also reflects her state of mind and her belief in order and discipline in life to counteract despair and confusion. (Berenson has obviously been complaining about his wife, Mary.)

> It is not Mary's fault, poor dear, to have had such an inheritance, & such a training – or want of it – but, oh, how grateful it makes me for any kind of discipline one has had, & how much more & more in love with the pondered, the weighted & measured science acquired painfully, drop by drop, grain by grain, in the laboratory of continual effort! After all, it is disconsecutiveness that does most of the mischief, isn't it? . . .
>
> How sorrow does *un*prepare one for joy. I feel it curiously just now in my numbness, my lack of reaction to the great good news of the last two or three days. I've never felt as tired & spent, not so much physically (for I'm much better) as mentally, & in my soul. So much of me is dead that I'm a little like a tree from where just one or two branches too many have been cut; & though one came to me from the dead I don't believe I would believe his message . . .
>
> The trouble with me is that my sorrows are real & solid & substantial, & I can lunch & dine with them daily.
>
> So ought my consolations to be (I mean as solid) dearest BB, with such friends as you & the one or two others in whom I really live and breathe. But they are so few, & the centre of their lives is elsewhere, necessarily.

In April 1913 she suffered a temporary disruption to one of her most valid friendships; that with Henry James, over a present of money to him on his seventieth birthday. She was deeply hurt over James's outrage at the idea of a gift of money; she wrote to Gaillard Lapsley on 13 april: 'There was nothing on earth I valued as much as his affection. I can never get over this.' James had been of great support to her with Teddy and had been present at the Mount during the Whartons' last stay there when Teddy had been at his most erratic. He had also been the recipient of her confidences over her affair with Morton Fullerton. Fortunately, her breach with James was soon healed.

For someone who valued continuity, tradition and order as deeply as Edith Wharton, the breaking of ties with the past in both her private world and the world at large must have been traumatic. The pain of this disruption was reflected in her health, with attacks of vertigo, hay fever and gastric disorders. In addition, her affair with Morton Fullerton had dwindled to an end during 1910 and she had been fifty years old in 1912. She can have had little expectation of building new close emotional ties, although Walter Berry remained in her life until his death in 1928. The bleakness and loneliness of her private life is undoubtedly reflected in her fiction of this period. In *Ethan Frome* (1911), *The Reef* (1912), and *The Custom of the Country* (1913), the main characters are notable for their loneliness. Ethan, Mattie and Zeena; Anna Leath, Darrow and

Sophy Viner; Undine Spragge and Ralph Marvell are all isolated by virtue of misjudgement or inadequacy.

6. Letter to W.C. Brownell (who took over at Scribner's) 27 July 1918.
7. Henry James in his Preface to *The Portrait of a Lady*, in attempting to recall 'the germ' of his idea for the novel, writes that:

> It must have consisted not at all in any conceit of a 'plot' . . . but altogether in the sense of a single character, the character and aspect of a particularly engaging young woman, to which all the elements of a 'subject', certainly of a setting, were to need to be superadded.

James remembers 'fondly' a remark he heard from 'the lips of Ivan Turgenieff in regard to his own experience of the usual origin of the fictive picture' which resembles strongly Edith Wharton's description of the origins of her novels:

> It began for him almost always with the vision of some person or persons, who hovered before him, soliciting him, as the active or passive figure, interesting him and appealing to him just as they were and by what they were.

This gave James:

> Higher warrant than I seemed then to have met for just that blest habit of one's own imagination, the trick of investing some conceived or encountered individual, some brace or group of individuals, with the germinal property and authority.

8. The name Caspar Levick, which occurs in the notebook, remains unaltered in the scenario and chapter summaries, but becomes Oscar Levick in the manuscript (p. 91), and is only returned to its original form by a manuscript alteration on Draft 2. Julia Birnam starts in the Notebook as Julia Wilshire, but is always referred to as Mrs Birnam from the scenario stage to Draft 2, while her husband Spofford – as he is in the drafts – had his Christian name changed to Power in the Notebook. The only other alterations of note are to Inez Clay, whose surname was changed from Beckford, and to Silmore, who is Sillamore in the first notes. The names Bowler Bush, the hero Richard Thaxter, Carmen Bliss and Uncles Horace Boole and Wayne Ketterick appear in the Notebook in their final form.
9. Letter to Bernard Berenson 18 November 1913 (I Tatti collection).
10. Between the scenario stage and the chapter summaries there are few changes except to the order of events. Book One remains unchanged. The first small change at the beginning of Book Two is that Dick's play has a name: 'The Duchess of Spartivento' (The Duke of Spartivento is Vance's rival for the affections of Floss Delaney in *The Gods Arrive*). In Chapter VIII a character appears, Garbish, theatrical impresario, who has not figured in the scenario. He is not developed in the final draft but appears simply as a name – 'the dread impresario' – the power behind

the Liberty theatre and Miss Inez Clay, 'the great Garbish' who 'at the last, had proved recalcitrant' (Dr 2) and 'had not seen his way to producing the play unassisted'. He sends his ambassador to tell Dick that 'it costs just as much money to produce elevating drama as the other kind, and the returns ain't as quick . . . If you can find a backer to put down ten thousand for you, Mr Garbish'll do the rest. *He* ain't afraid of risks – he *wants* to encourage art' (Dr 2).

From Chapter XI of the summaries up to Chapter XIX the order of events is changed: Dick is already doing 'hack' journalism before he meets Silmore and goes to Europe whereas in the scenario he is not reduced to this until he returns to New York and is rejected by Silmore as a 'failure'; in Chapter XIII Silmore's offer of the year abroad is not made until after the scene with Mrs Birnam's husband, while in the scenario he has already made the proposition and Dick then has to consider it in the light of the scene with the jealous husband. Curiously, the summary of Chapter XIII tells more about Dick's thoughts and feelings than the scenario: 'What must he do, what will be expected of him?', he 'loathes', 'feels he ought', 'dares not'. Chapters XIV to XVIII, on the other hand, are extremely briefly outlined. By Chapter XIX we gather that Dick has already married Rose before – or shortly after – returning to New York, whereas in the scenario he waits until he has a salary. In Chapter XXIV Dick's successful novel has been named 'John Santorin'. Finally, there is a note at the side of Chapter XXXVI: 'He decides to kill himself; & at that moment the thought of a big book comes to him, & he sits down and writes the scenario.'

11. In *BG* 116 she tells of the 'adjective hunts' that she carried out with Walter Berry on her manuscripts to the same effect.

Chapter Five

1. See *HM*, 63 and 69.
2. *Hudson River Bracketed*:
    Chapters 1–6 Vance's point of view; Chapters 7 and 8 Halo's point of view;
    Chapter 9 Vance's point of view; Chapter 10 Halo's point of view;
    Chapters 11–15 Vance's point of view; Chapter 16 Halo's point of view;
    Chapters 17 and 18 Vance's point of view; Chapters 19 and 20 Halo's point of view;
    Chapters 21–3 Vance's point of view; Chapter 24 (half-way) Halo's point of view;
    Chapters 24 (half-way) – 28 Vance's point of view; Chapter 29 Halo's point of view;
    Chapters 30–9 Vance's point of view; Chapters 40 and 41 Halo's point of view;
    Chapters 42–6 Vance's point of view.

The Gods Arrive

Chapter 1 Halo's point of view; Chapters 2 and 3 Vance's point of view;

Chapters 4–7 Halo's point of view; Chapter 8 Vance's point of view;

Chapters 9 and 10 Halo's point of view; Chapters 11–14 Vance's point of view;

Chapter 15 Halo's point of view; Chapters 16–29 Vance's point of view;

Chapters 30 and 31 Halo's point of view; Chapter 32 (half-way) Vance's point of view;

Chapters 32 (half-way) – 34 Halo's point of view; Chapters 35–40 Vance's point of view;

Chapter 41 Halo's point of view.

Bibliography

Aamons, Elizabeth (1980) *Edith Wharton's Argument with America*. Athens, Georgia: University of Georgia Press.

Askew, Melvin Wayne (1957) 'Edith Wharton's Literary Theory', unpublished dissertation, University of Oklahoma (Abstract DA 1957, XVII, 3009).

Auchincloss, Louis (1961) *Edith Wharton*. Minneapolis: University of Minnesota Press.

—— (1962) Afterword to *Hudson River Bracketed*. New York: New American Library of World Literature.

—— (1965) *The Edith Wharton Reader*. New York: Scribner's.

Beach, Joseph Warren (1932) *The Twentieth Century Novel: Studies in Technique*. New York: Appleton-Century, pp. 291–303, 311–14.

Bell, Millicent (1966) *Edith Wharton and Henry James*. London: Peter Owen.

—— (1957) 'Lady into Author: Edith Wharton and the House of Scribner', *American Quarterly* 9 (Fall), 295–315.

Berenson, Bernard (1949) *Sketches for a Self-Portrait*. New York: Pantheon.

Brown, E.K. (1962) 'Edith Wharton: The Art of the Novel', in Irving Howe (ed.) *Edith Wharton: Collected Essays*. Englewood Cliffs, NJ: Prentice-Hall.

Buitenhuis, Peter (1966) 'Edith Wharton and the First World War', *American Quarterly* 18 (Fall), 493–505.

Canby, H.S. (1948) 'Edith Wharton', in *Literary History of the United States*. London: Macmillan, Vol. II, 1209–11.

Chanler, Mrs Winthrop (1936) 'Winters in Paris', *Atlantic Monthly* 158, (Oct.), 476–80.

Coolidge, Olivia (1965) *Edith Wharton 1862–1937*. New York: Scribner's.

Gimbel, Wendy (1984) Edith Wharton: *Orphancy & Survival*. New York: Praegar.

Gleason, James Joseph (1969) 'After Innocence: the Later Novels of Edith Wharton', unpublished dissertation, Ohio State University (Abstract DA, XXX).

Goethe (1958) *The Great Writings of Goethe* (ed. Stephen Spender). New York: New American Library.

Goethe (1959) *Faust* Part Two. Harmondsworth: Penguin Books.

Greene, Graham (1951) *The End of the Affair*. Harmondsworth: Penguin Books.

Griffith, Grace (1965) *The Two Lives of Edith Wharton*. New York: Appleton-Century.

Grumbach, Doris (1973) 'Reconsideration: Edith Wharton', *New Review* 168, 29–30.

Hopkins, Viola (1958) 'The Ordering of Style of *The Age of Innocence*', *American Literature* 30, 345–57.

Howe, Irving (1962) 'The Achievement of Edith Wharton', Introduction to *Edith Wharton: A Collection of Critical Essays*. Englewood Cliffs, NJ: Prentice-Hall.

Howe, Irving (ed.) (1962) *Edith Wharton: Collection of Critical Essays*. Englewood Cliffs, NJ: Prentice-Hall.

James, Henry (1914) *Notes on Novelists, with Some Other Notes*. New York: Scribner's, pp. 353–5.

—— (1914) 'The Younger Generation', *Times Literary Supplement*, 2 April.

—— (1920) *The Letters of Henry James* (ed. Percy Lubbock). New York: Scribner's.

—— (1962) *The Art of the Novel. New York: Scribner's.*

Josipovici, Gabriel (1979) *The World and the Book*. London: Macmillan, pp. 179–200.

Kazin, Alfred (1942) *On Native Grounds*. New York: Reynal & Hitchcock, pp. 73–82.

Kellogg, Grace (1965) *The Two Lives of Edith Wharton: the Woman and Her World*. New York: Appleton-Century.

Koestler, Arthur (1964) *The Act of Creation*. London: Hutchinson.

La Guardia, Eric (1958) 'Edith Wharton on Critics and Criticism', *Modern Language Notes* (1976) 63 (Dec.), 587–9.

Lawson, Richard H. (1976) *Edith Wharton*. New York: Frederick Ungar.

Leach, Nancy R. (1957) 'Edith Wharton's Unpublished Novel', *American Literature* 30 (Mar.), 63–6.

Leavis, Q.D. (1938) 'Henry James's Heiress: The Importance of Edith Wharton', *Scrutiny* 7 (Dec.), 261–76.

Lewis, R.W.B. (1968) *The Collected Short Stories of Edith Wharton* Vol. II. New York: Scribner's.

—— (1975) *Edith Wharton: A Biography*. New York: Harper & Row.

Lindberg, Gary Hans (1967) 'Edith Wharton and the Rhetoric of Manners', unpublished dissertation, Stanford University, 1967 (Abstract DA, XXVIII, 4637A–8A).

Lovett, Robert M. (1925) *Edith Wharton*. New York: McBride.

Lubbock, Percy (1915) 'The Novels of Edith Wharton', *Quarterly Review* 224 (Jan.), 182–201.

—— (1947) *Portrait of Edith Wharton*. London: Jonathan Cape.

—— (1958) *The Craft of Fiction*. New York: Viking Press.

Lyde, Marilyn (1959) *Edith Wharton: Convention and Morality in the Work of a Novelist*. Norman OK: Oklahoma University Press, 1959.

Mariano, Nicky (1966) *Forty Years with Berenson*. London Harvard U.P., Chapter 5.

McDowell, Margaret (1976) *Edith Wharton*. Boston: Twayne.

Miller, Karl (1985) *Doubles*. Oxford: Oxford University Press, Chapter 13.

Nevius, Blake (1953) *Edith Wharton: a Study of her Fiction*. Berkeley and Los Angeles: University of California Press (2nd eds.).

Origo, Iris (1970) *Images and Shadows*. London: John Murray, pp. 23–26, 30–1.

Parrington, V.L. (1921) 'Our Literary Aristocrat', *The Pacific Review* (June).

Pitlick, Mary Louise (1965) 'Edith Wharton's Narrative Technique: the Major Phase', unpublished dissertation, University of Wisconsin, 1965 (Abstract DA, XXVI, 3347–8).

Plante, Patricia R. (1962) 'The Critical Reception of Edith Wharton's Fiction in America and England with an Annotated Enumerative Bibliography of Wharton Criticism from 1900 to 1961', unpublished dissertation, Boston University, 1962 (Abstract DA XXIII, 1706).

Poirier, Richard (1965) 'Edith Wharton and *The House of Mirth*', in Wallace Stegner (ed.) *The American Novel from James Fenimore Cooper to William Faulkner*. New York: Basic Books, pp. 117–32.

Ransom, John Crowe (1936) 'Characters and Character: a Note on Fiction', *American Review* 6 (Jan.), 271–88.

Russell, F.T. (1932) 'Edith Wharton's Use of Imagery', *English Journal* 21.

Semel, Sister Ann (1971) 'A Study of the Thematic Design in the Four Major Novels of Edith Wharton', unpublished dissertation, University of Notre Dame, (Abstract DA (32), 2702).

Trilling, Diana (1947) 'The House of Mirth' Revisited', *Harper's Bazaar* 81, (Dec.) 125–7, 181–6.

Trilling, Lionel (1956) 'The Morality of Inertia', in Robert McIver (ed.) *Great Moral Dilemmas*. New York: Harper & Bros.

Tuttleton, James W. (1968) 'Edith Wharton: Form and the Epistemology of Artistic Creation', *Criticism* 10 (Fall) 334–51.

—— (1973) 'Edith Wharton: Social Historian of Old New York', in *The Novel of Manners in America*. Chapel Hill: University of North Carolina Press, Chapter 5.

Tyler, William R. (1973) 'Personal Memories of Edith Wharton', *Proceedings of the Massachusetts Historical Society (85)*, 91–104.

Van Doren, Carl (1922) *Contemporary American Novelists, 1900–1920*. New York: Macmillan, pp. 95–104.

—— (1940) *The American Novel, 1789–1939*. New York: Macmillan, pp. 260–80.

Walton, Geoffrey (1970) *Edith Wharton: A Critical Interpretation*. Rutherford NJ: Fairleigh Dickinson University Press.

Warnock, Mary (1976) *Imagination*. London: Faber & Faber.

Wershoven, Carol (1982) *The Female Intruder in the Novels of Edith Wharton*. London and Toronto: Associated University Presses.

Whyte, L.L. (1962) *The Unconscious before Freud*. London: Tavistock.
Wilson, Edmund (1941) *The Wound and the Bow*. Boston: Houghton Mifflin, pp. 195–213.
—— (1950) *Classics and Commercials*. New York: Farrar, Straus, pp. 412–18.
Wolff, Cynthia Griffin (1977) *A Feast of Words: the Triumph of Edith Wharton*. New York: Oxford University Press.

Index